CANADA AND THE BURDEN OF UNITY

Canada and the Burden of Unity

EDITED BY
DAVID JAY BERCUSON

Macmillan of Canada

Canadian Cataloguing in Publication Data

Main entry under title:

Canada and the burden of unity

Includes bibliographical references.
ISBN 0-7705-1487-1 bd.   ISBN 0-7705-1488-X pa.

1. Federal-provincial relations (Canada) — Addresses, essays, lectures.* 2. Regionalism — Canada — Addresses, essays, lectures. 3. Canada — Economic conditions — Addresses, essays, lectures. I. Bercuson, David Jay, 1945-

JL27.C35   321'.02'0971   C77-001058-X

Printed in Canada for
The Macmillan Company of Canada Limited
70 Bond Street
Toronto, Ontario M5B 1X3

For Cheryl, Michael, and Sharon

Contents

CANADA AND THE BURDEN OF UNITY

Preface

This book is intended to go against the grain of Canadian history. The basic idea that hinterlands have common problems and that there is real value in exploring them on a comparative basis is not new but is still a novelty in Canada. The contributors to this volume hoped to make a beginning. Some will take umbrage at the theme and approach of the essays which follow, but it is our belief that Canada can only be strengthened by the kind of searching examination of basic issues which this book represents. A subject of this importance and scope is so broad, with so many facets, that it is impossible to touch every base in one small collection. We hope, however, that this book will be a start.

As with all works of this type, the help and cooperation of many people went into the final product: Virgil Duff of Macmillan; Diane Mew; Liesbeth von Wolzogen and the office staff of the University of Calgary History Department, especially Helen Nixon; the contributors; and my wife Cheryl who was so helpful in working out the idea and so encouraging in its execution.

DAVID JAY BERCUSON
Calgary, 1976

DAVID JAY BERCUSON

Canada's Burden of Unity: An Introduction

Canada is a country of regions. There is nothing new or extraordinary about this observation, and the fact is recognized, sometimes grudgingly, by academics, journalists, and politicians. Our trouble is that, having paid lip-service to the concept, too many Canadians who should know better wish regionalism would go away. If the stubborn regional identification of British Columbians, prairie Westerners, and Maritimers could only be melded with the all too powerful and sometimes parochial "Canadian" awareness of Ontarians, the land could be neatly split between the French and "English" of the bicultural illusion. That is the wish of some, but the ever-present reality is quite different. Regions exist, distinguished by geographical setting, economic role, history, culture, and even different ambitions for the same Canada to which they all belong. As J. M. S. Careless has so aptly phrased it, ". . . the experience of regionalism remains prominent and distinctive in Canadian history—and time has tended less to erode it than to develop it."[1]

Travel the length of this land along the thin spine of highway and steel which holds it together against the primeval power of the Precambrian shield, the awesome loneliness of endless wheatlands, and the terrifying majesty of the Rockies, and the "why" of regionalism becomes starkly apparent. Geographic determinants are basic, but in the course of Canadian political and economic development other factors of equal importance have been added. Colonies—Newfoundland, New Brunswick, Nova Scotia, the Canadas, British Columbia—existed before Confederation, the products of separate and distinct historical development. Confederation brought them together, and eventually gave political form to yet another great region—as the provinces of Manitoba, Saskatchewan, and Alberta were created—but it could not unite them spiritually. They had not really known each other and too often were cajoled into union by wily and ambitious local politicians, or were bludgeoned by the Colonial Office into an acceptance of the cold fact of British withdrawal from North America, or fell victim to the lure of a Canadian treasury ready and able to bail them out of their foolhardy railroad debts. Confederation was no marriage of love and affection; it was a union of convenience and, in the case of the Canadas, not even a union but a divorce.

There are probably as many definitions of regionalism as there are people defining, the most common being that which distinguishes five major areas in Canada: the Maritimes, Quebec, Ontario, the Prairies, and British Columbia. The power of Quebec votes and the necessity of the federal government to pay as much heed to Quebec as it does to Ontario reveals the existence of one region—Central Canada—with common characteristics. It is industrialized, populous, part of the St. Lawrence heartland, the holder of an absolute majority of seats in the House of Commons, and the major beneficiary of national economic, cultural, and social policies. The French-English contradiction which appears to separate Ontario from Quebec serves only to force even more federal attention towards this region, almost always at the expense of the West and the Maritimes. In like manner, the almost identical resource-extraction and provision roles forced on the Prairies and British Columbia by federal policies make these two "regions" far more alike than they are separate. The products are radically different, the Prairies supplying agricultural commodities, British Columbia minerals and lumber, but the part each plays in Confederation is essentially the same because the regional output is exported for processing. Here too one region can be seen to emerge from two when examined from the perspective of economic utility to the "national" purpose. Thus we are left with the Maritimes, Central Canada, and the West—two ends and a powerful, populous middle.

If Canadians were to finally accept regionalism as a fact of their national lives and use it as a foundation for the development of truly national policies and attitudes, it could well prove to be a blessing. Unfortunately, federal policies, the attitudes of Central Canadian governments, and the biases of so-called national institutions, such as the Canadian Broadcasting Corporation, have painted regionalism with the brush of divisiveness, disunity, and even treason. Influences tending to strengthen regional power are "balkanizing" while those working to increase the central power are "in the national interest." But this is true only if what is good for Central Canada is also good for Canada. The essays in this volume seriously question that assumption.

Central Canadian representation at Ottawa forces federal governments to identify with Ontario and Quebec first and foremost. This difficulty was forecast before Confederation by opponents of union in the Maritimes who envisaged rapid and continuous population growth in the Canadas and a relatively stable population in the Atlantic region. They believed that in not too many years their representatives at Ottawa would scarcely be able to make themselves heard amidst the Ontario and Quebec representatives. Though the imbalances never developed to the extent forecast (one New Brunswick newspaper saw 213 seats for Ontario and Quebec by 1901 versus 47 for the four Maritime provinces) they were and are serious enough nonetheless. Ontario and Quebec together have always held an absolute majority of seats, making it possible for a government to sit at Ottawa without one Western or Maritime representative. In a liberal democratic society it is hard to see any alternative.

The result has been predictable. Federal policies have served the interests of Central Canada. One obvious example, though by no means the only one, is the tariff. Since 1879, Canadians have been forced to shoulder a higher cost and a lower standard of living so that industries which probably should never have been established in the first place could start up behind the artificial walls of tariff protection. Instead of developing a few highly efficient and competitive specialties, as befits our small population, we developed a great many inefficient and uncompetitive industries. The benefits to Central Canada were obvious—jobs, markets for local farmers, profits for businessmen, shippers, and bankers—but the benefits for Maritimers and Westerners, if any, are hard to find. The ill effects abound: high prices for the manufactured products of Central Canada (added to by shipping costs) and the loss to East and West of significant commercial intercourse with New England and the northwestern areas of the United States.

The initiation of a protective tariff, which has created far more benefits for Central Canadians than Maritimers or Westerners, is only one stark example of what happens when there is no effective guardian of all regional interests at work within the federal structure. Each region must be protected because what is in the interest of one is not necessarily in the interest of another, particularly in a country covering as great an area and spanning so many different geographic, climatic, cultural, and economic environments. This is a truism, oft repeated, which is used to justify the existence of federalism in Canada. But federalism, which was constructed primarily to preserve and protect regional interests, while at the same time uniting British North Americans into one national entity, cannot work if it is to be undermined by the belief that what suits a simple majority suits all. It is precisely such thinking, however, which surfaces so often on economic, cultural, social, educational, and political questions. John A. Macdonald wanted one central government in Ottawa which would administer the entire country without interference from local provincial authorities, but others, Maritimers and French Canadians, foresaw the disastrous consequences such a constitutional structure would create. They opted for federalism to protect not only cultures but regions. But the system they developed contained few real safeguards. It produced, instead, an inevitable growth of provincial power to accomplish this very task while it allowed Central Canada to use the federal government to force Maritimers and Westerners into a mould cast in Ontario.

Under these circumstances the "limited identities" discussed by Careless and Ramsay Cook[2] flourished and were strengthened by the growth of mutual suspicions and rivalries. To compound the situation, and perhaps to solidify it into permanent shape, the federal government, endowed with the massive political, fiscal, and economic powers given it by the British North America Act, began, soon after Confederation, to establish long-range developmental goals for its national charge. Here, however, a Conservative party with an ideological leaning towards the use of centralized power, led by a prime minister who had wished the provinces to be no more than glorified municipalities, tended to identify the interests of the great majority of voters living in Central Canada with the desires of all Canadians. The tendency was natural for a party which derived the greater part of its support in Ontario and Quebec, and it was even reflected in the writings and pronouncements of Canada First, a group professing to espouse nationalism, but actually voicing the concerns of Ontario parochialism. When Macdonald and his Conservatives embarked on the fulfillment of a national policy in 1879 the problems of centralization were compounded by a program designed to hold the resource hinterlands of Atlantic and Western Canada in permanent fiefdom to the intended industrial heartland of Ontario and Quebec.

These federal policies, far from breaking down the barriers of regionalism, imposed differences of role on the Maritimes and the West, and forced their economies into rigid patterns subservient and contributing to the power of Central Canada. The tariff, the railway, and the political muscle of Ottawa assured the continued existence of regionalism and the certainty of regional discontent. The Maritimes and the West could do little about this "no win" situation at the federal level. They could not defend or assert themselves within the cabinet and party structure at Ottawa because a vicious circle of circumstance assured them of continuing weakness of representation in the halls of the federal government.

Industrialization and population growth are necessarily connected. Canada was destined by geography and federal policy to have an industrialized centre and an agricultural and resource-extraction periphery. Population growth in the outlying regions has never kept pace with that of Central Canada because the Maritimes and the West are not industrialized. The Maritimes and the West are not strongly represented at Ottawa because of the relatively low population. National growth might have been more even, if federal policies had been designed to help hinterlands overcome geographic handicaps, but the federal government has always been more representative of the desires and ambitions of Central Canada than the Maritimes and the West together. Central Canada is where the votes are and where elections are won and lost; this was true at Confederation and it remains true today. The federal government does not aim to stimulate industrialization in the peripheral regions, and one continuing result will be slow or no population growth. The payoff, the bribe, is our institutionalized government-to-government welfare policy of equalization payments: a Band-Aid program used to substitute for radical surgery. Since the hinterland regions are at a permanent disadvantage in federal politics they turn to their provincial governments for protection. The identification of some Canadians with their own regions, as much as or perhaps more than their identification with the whole nation, is a fact of Canadian life that will not easily be made to go away.

It would be a mistake to conclude that no effective guardian of regional interests was ever intended or created: the Maritimes would never have entered Confederation without such protection. The institution designed to protect such interests was the Senate, but because it was appointive in a society with a growing democratic consciousness it was handicapped from the beginning and has become the appendix of the Canadian body politic. Though the Senate is almost always remembered as the guardian of the rich minority, to paraphrase Macdonald, it was intended by its defenders to be the one area of the federal government to represent the interests of the regions and guard them against a too zealous use of centralized power. This is why it was given equal regional representation, not unlike the principle followed in the United States Senate. It is also one reason for Newfoundland bowing out of the Confederation negotiations in 1866 when it discovered that it would not be granted senatorial representation additional to that being allotted New Brunswick, Nova Scotia, and Prince Edward Island. It also explains why the Quebec Conference of 1866 devoted so much time to discussing senatorial representation.[3]

The Senate, however, was also saddled with other tasks and was handicapped by its unrepresentative nature. It was supposed to ride herd on the potentially democratic, and therefore dangerous, Commons and was to be appointed from amongst Canada's wealthy. Even more crucial, its members were to be picked, not by the provincial governments, as the United States Senate was then appointed by the states, but by the federal government. The Senate could not reflect regional interests while it stood above the workings of the democratic process in a world where the principle of appointment was increasingly unpopular. It inevitably became the Valhalla of old and tired political warhorses.

The Senate's lack of effectiveness as guardian of regional interests forced the provincial governments to the fore. There was simply no alternative. An enlightening comparison with the United States system of government shows the opposite—federal power increased, state power withered while the United States Senate, an elected body (since 1911) which balances the different regional interests in the republic, has never ceased to be a vigorous and powerful part of government. State governments have withered for a variety of reasons, but surely one reason is that the Senate is the most effective guardian of regional interests in the entire American governmental system. The Senate plays a crucial and sometimes dominant role in making federal policy, but because of its composition and manner of election it guards the interests of the states and regions from which its members come. Since no such body exists in Canada the provincial governments must do the job. But they are decidedly imperfect instruments for protecting regional interests.

The British North America Act bestows upon the federal government the power to regulate all interprovincial and international trade and commerce, and the use of the airwaves; unlimited powers to set and enforce tariffs and taxes; and the sole authority to set and regulate interprovincial airline, rail, and truck traffic. If federalism is to have any meaning as a system in which various states or provinces are united for common goals and purposes, provincial governments must have more limited areas of responsibility and should not be allowed to encroach on areas of truly national jurisdiction. This is why the provincial governments are imperfect guardians of regional interests. Those policies which benefit one region to the detriment of another, by their very nature, originate in the federal government and are usually beyond the constitutional reach of provincial authorities. If Canada contained a relatively balanced population across the regions there would be little danger of such policies arising because federal parties would have to woo support from all areas of the country or lose office. When most Canadians live in one region, however, this imperative does not exist. This is why no amount of protest from the West or the Maritimes, expressed through third parties, provincial governments, or in a federal party caucus has ever brought about a fundamental change in any national policy.

Provincial governments have grown more powerful. They have benefited from decades of court decisions which eroded important areas of section 91 of the British North America Act, particularly the "peace, order and good government" clause, and enhanced key areas of section 92, especially "property and civil rights." This process began even before the first interprovincial conference in 1887, when four provinces launched the first concerted attack against the federal power, and it enables them to sit today at numerous federal-provincial conferences and force Ottawa to share decision-making in areas such as welfare policy. The growth of provincial power, however, has been unbalanced, arising piecemeal from court decisions, and has never infringed on areas clearly within the purview of a national government, such as trade, transportation, and broadcasting.

The federal government has not been completely insensitive to the problems of Westerners and Maritimers. The record shows federal initiation of the Crow's Nest Pass Agreement to assure low freight rates on grain, and federal activities to alleviate the plight of western farmers during the depression of 1929–39 which went far to restoring the wheat economy. Federal experimental farms, research programs, and other projects have definitely benefited Westerners, and similar programs, generally aiming towards rural stabilization and industrial diversification, have aided the Atlantic region. But this is no more than should be expected of a government looking to the general welfare of all. The crucial distinction between these programs and those such as the National Policy which placed hinterland regions at a disadvantage to Central Canada is that the latter became fundamentally tied in with federal concepts of national growth and development and remained unchanged despite all kinds of pressures and special pleadings. The former types of programs did not detrimentally affect Central Canadian interests and actually worked to their benefit as well as to the benefit of Westerners and Maritimers. How could the National Policy work if it was not based on a healthy wheat economy? Thus the changes necessary to create real balance in this country—in industry, resource development, broadcasting, transportation— have never been made. The equation is fundamental: every new steel plant established in Nova Scotia and every new plastics plant built in Alberta takes potential jobs from Central Canada.

Though emphasis is usually placed on industrial development, or the lack of it, to illustrate regional disparity, national broadcast policies are an equally good example of regional discrimination. The Canadian Broadcasting Corporation has an important and unique task—guarding our cultural heritage and explaining us to ourselves. It is difficult to see how this can be done as long as the corporation continues to dictate taste and ideas from Toronto. At the very least, the corporation's task would assume the existence of important regional broadcasting centres, each turning out a significant amount of programming to serve the region and to be transmitted to other parts of Canada. Expensive? Of course; but a price we must pay for national unity and understanding. The point is that federal policies must be developed, at whatever cost, to help the outlying regions overcome the disadvantages of geography so that their citizens, their workers, farmers, bankers, businessmen, and industrialists, enjoy the same privileges as Central Canadians. It has always been difficult for Albertans to understand why it is a national tragedy if Quebeckers pay high prices for western petroleum products when they must pay high prices for automobiles, finished steel products, electronic equipment, etc., because of freight charges and tariffs.

Most of these problems, these flaws in Confederation, have been admitted but underplayed by Canadian scholars and politicians more interested in the greater symphony of "national unity." As Ramsay Cook pointed out, the preoccupation of the English-Canadian historian with the problems and prospects of Canadian survival leads him to expound upon "the virtue of national unity" and to make "present objectives the standard by which he judges past actions."[4] A brief look at some of our leading texts bears this out. In *Colony to Nation,* A. R. M. Lower concluded his story of the 1887 Provincial Conference, in which the premiers of Manitoba, Ontario, Quebec, and Nova Scotia demanded curtailment of certain federal powers and a more important role for the provinces, with the lament that "never before or since has Canada reached so low a state; never has there been so little evidence among its people of national spirit."[5] He was, of course, also referring to the English-French hatred generated by the Riel affair, but his lumping of the Provincial Conference with the riots and racial hatred which accompanied Riel's execution reveals his bias. Edgar McInnis in *Canada,* asserted that the long process of British judicial interpretation which eroded federal power created results, which "were of the gravest consequence for Canada's future."[6] W. L. Morton, in *The Kingdom of Canada,* observed that the prime task of "national statesmanship" after the 1921 federal election was "to restore the unity of purpose from which Confederation had sprung."[7] Donald Creighton, in *Canada's First Century,* placed the beginnings of the provincial-rights movement in a chapter entitled "Times of Troubles."[8] To him this new political trend was an obstacle to Macdonald's idea of national unity, not unlike the difficulties over the Canadian Pacific Railway and Louis Riel.

E. R. Forbes and T. W. Acheson explain what the Maritimes needed protection against. Forbes describes the crucial role played by misguided transportation policies in undermining the economy of the Maritimes after the First World War. In the first decades after Confederation, the Intercolonial Railway had created a de facto regional transportation policy which took into account the nature of the area's economy and which was not based upon the assumption that rate structures operative in Ontario must necessarily be applied to Nova Scotia or New Brunswick. The policy was beneficial for the commerce and industry of the region because it was based on realities rather than theoretical symmetry. But as the Maritime area lost power politically its ability to defend this special arrangement declined and the railway was forced to accept federal decisions aimed at instituting just such a symmetry. The result was disastrous for economies already in trouble. T. W. Acheson shares the assumption that there was nothing "natural" or inevitable about the decline of industry in the Maritime region. He demonstrates that thriving concerns were taken over and then closed down by Central Canadian companies, forcing a decline in living standards. One result is that the Maritimes became one vast recipient of government handouts, in the form of welfare or civil service jobs. Acheson stresses the startling fact that government has become the largest employer in the region and concludes this has helped destroy individual self-sufficiency and initiative.

T. D. Regehr's essay is a mirror to Forbes's. He tackles the problem of western transportation difficulties and shows how federally conceived policies were disastrous to the region. He describes the birth of the concept of "fair discrimination," based on the lack of western competition and the belief that the c. p. r. was entitled to discriminate against the West in its freight charges in return for its very presence at a time when its western operation was not highly profitable. Efforts by Westerners to undermine this policy were not successful because they simply did not have the political muscle. When, at a later time, the Canadian Northern Railway began to provide competition for the c. p. r. the situation improved, but this was offset by the federal government's support for a wholly new Grand Trunk Pacific Railway. Regehr concludes by pointing to the hard facts: there is still no competition for rail transportation in the West; industry, which is not protected by the Crow's Nest Rates, suffers from a discriminatory rate structure; the entire rail system on the prairies is obsolete and in need of rationalization but is inextricably intertwined with the quality of rural life and the existence of small communities. His solution is strong medicine: if the federal government will not create a custom-made, rational, western transportation policy, the provincial governments will have to do it, because, quite simply, it has to be done.

This book is also about unity but its perspective is different. This is anti-national history: the dominant theme of these essays is that the sacrifices called for in the name of "national unity" have taken a heavy toll in the hinterland regions and no real national unity can be attained until national priorities have been rearranged. This book is not about separatism, but it is based on the belief that there is a middle ground between advocating the destruction of Confederation and having blind faith in unity. Here there is careful and detailed analysis of some of the significant problems that Confederation caused, or rather, that were caused in the name of Confederation. The purpose is to show clearly that "national unity" has created burdens that have not been equitably borne and serious national difficulties that have never been tackled.

Paul Phillips, for example, presents a compelling case that one major reason for the deep penetration of multinational corporations into the Canadian economy has been "national" policies that ignored the reality of regionalism and the differences in the regional economies. As long as such policies are based on the assumption that Canada is a single, viable, policy-making unit, he asserts, multinational penetration will continue and we will lose more control over our economy. This points to the ironic conclusion that in creating a Central Canadian bias in the national economy, our strength to resist foreign domination was weakened and not enhanced. Phillips suggests that government must play a more positive role in the reallocation of capital investment into the regions.

Carman Miller points to another irony: Maritime union, as envisaged by the leaders of the Atlantic colonies in the early 1860s, was not a pipe dream, but a logical political culmination of the ties that had been developing on several levels for many decades. But Maritime unity was abandoned in the move to Confederation and the Maritimes were probably the poorer for it in the long run. Could Confederation have come about if the Atlantic colonies had joined into a single colony? Probably, given the pressures of the British Colonial Office, but the single Maritime province thus created would have had a much stronger voice in the creation of national policies, and would have been better able to protect itself in the decades that followed. The task today is to develop substitutes for the union that never existed.

Colin Howell and David Smith focus on politics. Howell presents a case study in provincial protest. His story, however, is not one of "cranky" regionalism, but reflects how Nova Scotians reacted to an increasingly centralized federal system that they believed to be inequitable. His conclusion is that Nova Scotian protest was motivated not by a desire to destroy Confederation but by a desire to create a more equal and fair federal system. This story points back to Ramsay Cook's conclusions about English-Canadian historians and their preoccupation with survival. John A. Macdonald and some of the framers of Confederation conceived of a highly centralized federal system since they could not have legislative union. But was that concept one that would be beneficial to the new nation they were creating? If not, surely there is nothing sacred about attempts to defend that concept and nothing sacrilegious about efforts to alter it. Mercier, Mowatt, et al. may have been far wiser in their assessment of what Canada really needed than Macdonald. This would put Nova Scotia's attempts to force a restructuring of Canadian federalism in a different light.

David Smith tackles the tricky problem of the West's search for power in Confederation in light of the realities of prairie political history. Power is in the hands of the federal Liberal party, and since the West will probably continue to reject the Liberals for some time, how can policies equitable to the West be evolved? His answer points to the concept of devolution: the creation of agencies with quasi-executive power delegated from the federal government which would operate from within each region. Devolution would give the West some real control of policy implementation and might well allay the intense distrust of the federal government that has built up over the years.

These essays cover only a small part of the difficulties of regional inequity. They refer only obliquely to British Columbia and ignore difficulties such as those caused by a lack of regional input to federal cultural policy. The collection is not meant to be an exhaustive survey of the problems of regionalism and federalism but to show that the federal style that exists in Canada has created major problems that are still largely ignored, though lip service may be paid to finding solutions. These problems exist primarily because Ontario and Quebec are the major population centres and preoccupy the federal government.

What emerges from this book is a picture of the power of Central Canada, manifest through the federal government and other "national" institutions, which has created regional disparity and imposed its own version of national character and ambitions on Westerners and Maritimers. This process has continued virtually unabated since Confederation and shows no sign of slackening. Is there yet hope for the development of a federal style that will recognize the uniqueness of Canada's regions and not sacrifice the well-being of less populated areas?

One solution is to restructure the Senate, making it an elective body and providing for an equal number of senators from each province or perhaps region (if a common definition of region can be agreed upon). This is indeed radical surgery but it would solve the major problems of regional inequities without further undermining federal power. Such a body would have a powerful voice in the creation of national policies because it would be an important part of the federal decision-making apparatus. It would also be a true barometer of regional feelings, and prime ministers and cabinets would be forced to take its regionally balanced character into consideration when making policy. At the same time the propensity for regional discontent to be moulded by and voiced through provincial governments would be lessened because the Senate would have a hand in making those very policies which are the most responsible for regional inequities but over which provincial governments have no control.

At the same time, however, Senate reform would run into severe difficulties and is not a realistic proposal. An elected Senate would be far different from the "rubber stamp" upper house we now have and might seriously hamper the operation of the prime minister and his cabinet, who must continue to be chosen largely from the Commons and operate in it. Should the Senate and the Commons have different political majorities the difficulties of government might prove insurmountable. Perhaps more salient is the unlikelihood of a group of politicians in the Commons creating, by their own hands, a powerful rival in the Senate. Other problems of a constitutional nature would also come to the fore: should the Senate have a strictly fixed term or should it be elected when the Commons is elected and sit only as long as the Commons sits? Should senators sit in cabinets? Should prime ministers be chosen from the Senate? The difficulties appear endless, but the Canadian upper house was gradually becoming an elected body prior to Confederation. Canadian legislators of that day saw no problem in grafting an elected upper house onto the British parliamentary system.

Other solutions would involve enhancement of provincial power. It has frequently been observed in recent years that the federal-provincial conference has become a de facto instrument of Canadian government. This is all to the good, but such conferences are usually held at the instigation of the federal government and are used only to solve difficulties which arise over matters of finance or programs which override jurisdictions. If such conferences were called on a regular systematic basis, and provided for direct federal consultation with the governments of those regions most directly affected by particular policies, they would come closer to solving problems of regional disparity and inequity of treatment. Perhaps provincially appointed representatives of a permanently sitting national equivalent of the International Joint Commission might be given the authority to consult with the federal government, or even have a veto over certain federal policies.

Finally, whatever solution is chosen, all facilities which purport to serve national interests should be decentralized and have regional head offices capable of running local operations but which would remain under the general authority of national head offices in Ottawa or elsewhere. This should apply to departments of the federal government such as manpower, industry, trade and commerce, as well as Crown corporations such as the Canadian Broadcasting Corporation, Canadian National Railways, and Air Canada. It would certainly be more in the national interest if each region could boast a major C.B.C. broadcast production centre.

Should most of these ideas prove Utopian it is surely not too much to demand that prime ministers use greater discretion in building cabinets than they have recently. After Confederation the cabinet quickly emerged as a guardian of regional interests as forecast by Christopher Dunkin in the Canadian Confederation debates in 1865. In the West, as David Smith points out, this practice defused much regional discontent but has been abandoned in recent decades. A more balanced approach to cabinet construction will not solve any fundamental problems but could put an onus on ministers representing peripheral regions to take stronger positions in favour of their constituents. Perhaps political affiliation should be ignored in extraordinary circumstances to entice strong men into a federal cabinet which would not otherwise contain a balanced regional representation because of imbalances in the Commons.

What is important is not the particular solution but the realization that there is a problem to be solved. Once a difficulty such as a discriminatory freight-rate structure is isolated, it becomes relatively simple to put forth possible solutions. Our major problem is that regional inequity is either not recognized as being particularly dangerous to Canada or is considered unsolvable because of fundamental determinants such as climate or geography. Though regional inequity has been one of the most enduring features of Confederation, it has also been one of the most ignored.

Regional inequity is a serious problem and imposes tremendous burdens upon the Maritimes and the West. The Maritimes have suffered from a lower standard of living, higher unemployment, cultural isolation, and depopulation for decades. Their unevenly developed economies depend largely on market farming, lumbering, fishing, and government handouts. The spectre of separatism first arose in the Maritimes, not in Quebec, and the continuous problems of poverty and unemployment have forced tens of thousands to "go down the road," generally to Ontario or to the United States. Ottawa has never been slow to pour hundreds of millions of dollars into welfare programs and equalization payments, but it has not been willing to go to the root of the problem by changing cultural and economic policies which would bring the Atlantic region into the mainstream of Canadian society. To this day there languishes in the Maritimes ill will towards "Canada" and a belief that Confederation was a bad deal which worked to the advantage of one party alone. The burdens placed on Western Canada have been better known because they have created special kinds of political protest: Social Credit, Progressivism, the Cooperative Commonwealth Federation. Farmers' complaints about tariffs and railway rates are as much a part of the western scene as the spectacular thunderstorms of July. Other problems are less known but have been equally serious. Western businessmen have always been forced to try to overcome high transportation costs in their fight against eastern and American competition. One result has been the emergence of a branch-plant economy paying the kind of homage to eastern business that many Canadian commercial and industrial interests pay to the United States. Two western provinces are now considered "have" provinces—Alberta and British Columbia—but they achieved this status only by extracting and selling (giving away?) non-renewable resources.

Finally there is the less materialistic, but no less real, burden of being ignored, misunderstood, stereotyped, and patronized by Central Canadians. Unless these situations are made to change and these burdens finally lifted from the shoulders of Westerners and Maritimers, Canada will not be a country with any singleness of purpose—and this is where the most dangerous threats to national unity will come from.

The key to success can lie only with the realization that federalism and regionalism are not incompatible. That federalism in Canada must be built upon the recognition of regional equality. The essays which follow point in greater detail to serious difficulties which have always stood in the path of such equality and indicate solutions compatible with our federal system. They may not be the right ones, they may not even be wholly practical, but if they force Canadians to begin to think seriously about this most difficult of problems, they will have accomplished a great deal. It is about time we tried to lay these burdens of unity down.

NOTES

1. J.M.S. Careless, "Limited Identities in Canada," *Canadian Historical Review* (March 1969), pp. 1-10.
2. Ibid., p. 1.
3. P.B. Waite, *The Life and Times of Confederation,* (Toronto, 1962), pp. 89-90.
4. Ramsay Cook, "La Survivance English-Canadian Style," in *The Maple Leaf Forever* (Toronto, 1971), p. 163.
5. A.R.M. Lower, *Colony to Nation* (Toronto, 1946), p. 387.
6. Edgar McInnis, *Canada* (Toronto, 1969), p. 419.
7. W.L. Morton, *The Kingdom of Canada* (Toronto, 1970), p. 437.
8. D.G. Creighton, *Canada's First Century* (Toronto, 1970), pp. 46-49.

PAUL PHILLIPS

National Policy, Continental Economics, and National Disintegration

Regionalism has always been a central characteristic of the Canadian economy and a dominant Canadian political issue. It fuelled the drive to Confederation in 1867, the rise and consolidation of western protest movements throughout the twentieth century, and the political repudiation of the federal Liberal party in the early 1970s throughout much of the Canadian hinterland. Why have the country's legislators never come to grips with this divisive issue? The purpose of this paper is to suggest an answer.

In simple terms it will be argued that Confederation was the culmination of a group of policies (which we now call the National Policy) designed to mould a country out of several disparate regions as a defence against American expansionism. The existence of Canada as a political unit attests to the initial success of the original National Policy. But economic and political realities have changed, and these policies have ceased to be relevant to the problems of the second half of the twentieth century. The assumption that Canada exists as a single, independent, economic policy-making unit is, as one economist has recently written, the "Canadian Fallacy."[1] Instead, the national presence in policy initiatives has largely been replaced by the hegemony of the multinational corporation and by continental integration. "The Canadian economy must be studied explicitly as a regional sector (or rather, as a number of regional sectors) of the North American economy."[2]

The significance of this change is that the Canadian government has lost the policy tools to attack the problem of regional disparity, and without the active participation of the central government the hinterland regions are unable to combat the economic forces that produce and reinforce these disparities. A first step, therefore, must be for Canada itself to regain control of its own economic policies by the implementation of a new national policy.

The National Policy was "collectively that group of policies and instruments which were designed to transform the British North American Territories of the mid-nineteenth century into a political and economic unit."[3] H. G. Aitken interprets this Canadian policy as a defence of British North America against the political and economic expansionism of American "manifest destiny." It was also a policy conceived and implemented by a predominantly commercial elite, located in the metropolitan centres of Central Canada along the St. Lawrence River system, to direct economic activity on an east-west axis so that this elite might control a greater volume of commerce and repair its sagging fortunes.[4]

In these terms, the National Policy was undoubtedly successful. An independent political unit or nation was formed, and, after the western frontier was filled and began exporting grain to Europe, the complementarity of the regions was demonstrated, although not without cost to the West. There can be little doubt that the leaders of Central Canada thought of the West as a hinterland to be developed to ensure the viability of the central region. It is amply demonstrated by the national government's determination to control prairie land resources to facilitate and pay for the western expansion of British North America. Thus, the National Policy—east-west railways to a settled resource hinterland protected by a comprehensive tariff system—was successful within the framework of the period. It was extended, again successfully, to integrate the great mining frontier of the time, in southeastern British Columbia, into the Canadian commercial system.[5]

The National Policy tariff, which effectively drew a line

across the continent over which trade would pass only with difficulty, was central to the whole concept. The barrier to free importation of manufactured goods, designed as it was to promote east-west commerce, was effective. But it also induced American industrial capital to cross the border to serve the Canadian market. In Western Canada, the results could have been predicted. The farmer had to sell his output, mainly grain, on an unprotected (European) international market, but had to buy his finished goods on a highly protected domestic market increasingly dominated by American manufacturers. What is significant, of course, is that the western producer had no control over either his market or his supplier. He was forced to accept both the competitive insecurities of the international grain system and the protected monopoly prices of the domestic market. Thus a grievance was created.

The tariff was only one of several difficulties for the West. The monopoly power vested in the Canadian Pacific Railway, owned and controlled in Central Canada, and dominion control of prairie crown lands were continuing sources of protest. Central Canada was maintaining control of the dominant prairie natural resource—land—in order to finance a centrally controlled railway. Only in 1929, when almost all of the productive land was alienated to private ownership and the wheat economy had ceased its expansive phase and was faced with depression, drought, and contraction, did Crown land revert to the prairie provinces.

The National Policy, therefore, fits into the metropolis-hinterland mould. A Central Canadian coalition, composed of a predominantly mercantile elite, with support from a small core of Canadian and American industrial capitalists and a growing number of industrial workers, created a resource hinterland to save themselves from economic decline. In this it was a success. The c.p.r., the Bank of Montreal, American subsidiary manufacturers, all prospered; as indeed did the satellite merchants, grain handlers, and wholesale traders, particularly in Winnipeg. So, periodically, did many farmers. But caught between the fluctuating world grain prices and more stable finished-goods prices, the western producer suffered wide variations in real income.[6]

The reaction of the western primary producers was often political protest. The same reaction occurred among the workers in the resource industries in British Columbia and Alberta. V. C. Fowke suggests that the adoption of a second national policy based on the extension of welfare measures, agricultural stabilization, and the adoption of monetary policy for purposes of income stabilization was the federal reaction to the distress of the hinterland regions.[7] It is questionable whether these measures should be recognized as a comprehensive national policy. In the first place, the establishment of old age pensions, family allowances, unemployment insurance, agricultural stabilization programs (including the Wheat Board), and the control of money supply and interest rates through the creation of the Bank of Canada may be accredited to ad hoc responses to political protest movements or to economic crises engendered by depression or war. Only in the postwar green paper on employment might one discern elements of a conscious "national policy." Even the more recent expansions of welfare provisions, such as hospital and medical insurance, were a response to initiatives by the government of Saskatchewan, not conscious directives of economic or stabilization policy.[8]

Whether or not Canada ever had a second national policy is, however, no longer important because the contemporary economy is simply not responsive to the kind of economic policies that Fowke is concerned with. The rise of the continental North American economy and the multinational corporation has, in the absence of compensating revisions in national policy, reduced the Canadian economy to being regions of the American economy. Fiscal policy, governing taxation and government expenditures, and monetary policy, controlling credit and interest rates which are designed to stabilize the national economy and reduce the uneven regional burdens of cyclical economic fluctuations, have become largely impotent. Similarly, regional development policies pursued by provincial and federal governments are also effectively neutralized.

Canadian economic performance, over the last half century at least, has almost directly followed that of the United States. This is a natural consequence of the integration of Canadian and American markets, in particular the capital market—the market for funds to finance industrial and commercial investment—and the rise in prominence of the multinational corporation. Because American influence overwhelmingly dominates, Canada has little policy leverage.

Consider, for instance, a situation wherein Canada would wish to pursue a more expansionary monetary policy than that of the United States by lowering interest rates. Multinational corporations and other financial institutions, through subsidiaries in Canada, would automatically transfer borrowings to the cheapest (i.e., the Canadian) market. The increased demand for Canadian funds would then drive Canadian interest rates back up as long as there were no direct controls on the flow of capital across the border. Such a result would not undermine Canadian policy if enough Canadian funds were available to satisfy the demands of American borrowers. In fact, interest rates in that country would decrease in that case. But the relative size of the two economies is paramount. The net effect of the initial Canadian move would be totally negated by the American reaction defeating Canada's attempt to control its interest rates. As David Rutenberg notes, "to the extent that the company can move money between nations, it can stand aloof from the monetary policy of individual nations and raise capital from the cheapest source anywhere."[9]

Fiscal policy also tends to be neutralized in a similar way. Assume that the Canadian government would wish to dampen inflation by increasing corporate income taxes. Integrated multinational companies can, in the absence of direct controls, by internal bookkeeping, shift their profits to other countries. This is done by altering transfer prices, the prices firms charge themselves for management fees, technology, semi-processed goods, machinery, and other internal costs. The purpose is to make the profits appear in the country with the lowest corporate tax. This means that the firms which suffer most from the increased taxes of a tight fiscal policy are the wholly Canadian companies who are in competition with the multinationals. As Andreas Papandreou has noted, a multinational "has capabilities of minimizing its global tax bill in ways not available to national companies."[10] This produces relatively poorer performance by Canadian firms and makes them susceptible to take-over bids by the multinationals, while it has little effect on the level of multinational operations. Similarly, if the United States adopts a different policy than Canada the process acts in reverse. But the important point is that, at present, Canada has only two options: it can accept that U.S. policy will be the dominant influence in the determination of the performance of the Canadian economy, or it can attempt to counteract this influence by adopting virtually identical fiscal policies. A Hobson's choice!

The limits to our economic policy options are a result of the integration of our economy with that of the U.S. and the size of the latter, along with the immediacy of the feedback of economic influences between the two countries through the agency of the multinational corporation and the free flow of capital. Our autonomy would not be lost, however, if economic relations between the U.S. and Canada were not so pervasive; that is, if Canada had many countries with which to interact. This, of course, is not the case. On the trade side of the picture, approximately a quarter of Canada's gross national product enters foreign trade, a high percentage in comparative world terms. Of this amount, between two-thirds and three-quarters is trade with the United States. There is thus little diversity to our trade flows.[11] On the capital side, foreign investment is substantial, even dominant, in many industries, particularly resources, and manufacturing. American capital accounts for approximately 80 per cent of this.[12]

An examination of the interconnections between regionalism, the National Policy, and continental integration reveals why, if the problem of regionalism is to be seriously attacked, it is first necessary to re-establish Canadian national control. The first National Policy was explicitly based on the integration of regions with diverse natural products into the international market. This was to be done through the instrument of the commercial-industrial system of Central Canada. But as Canadian regions became integrated, they became increasingly sensitive to fluctuations in these international markets where Canadian policy-makers could not exert any stabilizing influence. Moreover, the structure of the domestic economy and the influence of the National Policy tariffs continued to transfer the most serious effects of externally generated instabilities onto the resource hinterland regions, while the industrial heartland was protected by greater diversity and the tariffs which limited foreign competition. National welfare programs and agricultural stabilization policies have compensated to some extent for this uneven distribution of the economic benefits of the National Policy, but the problem remains.

The first National Policy was directed to the international grain market. However, wheat has ceased to be the driving force behind Canadian growth; it has been replaced by a number of new staple industries—pulp and paper, mining, petroleum, hydroelectric energy, and forest products. Nevertheless, the continuing dependence of Canadian staple exports on the American market or on multinational corporations perpetuates the regional impotence to combat externally generated instability and exploitation. The new staples are not sold in the same kind of competitive market that characterized the traditional grain markets, with thousands of farmers and numerous countries participating. No single government could control total supply in the world market, so that droughts, crop failures, or bumper harvests meant wide swings in price and income. In contrast, the new staples are characteristically controlled by large, multinational firms which individually can have some effect on price by restricting their levels of output. These firms do not have to accept the dictates of a free market. This may be particularly true if the firm is only one of many subsidiaries of a parent which buys all of its subsidiary's output for further manufacture and sale in a non-competitive market.

Why does this new structure not lessen the instabilities in the resource regions? In the first instance, fluctuations in prices of primary products are much greater than is the case with the products of secondary manufacturing. Secondly, the amount of investment per job is generally considerably greater in the new staple industries than in secondary manufacturing. This heavy investment comes from a variety of sources, not only for the basic extraction facility (e.g., a mine) but also for housing, schools, and other establishments that must accompany the development or expansion of a new resource-based town. This increases the instability of the construction industry in the hinterland region.[13] Thirdly, Canadian staples must compete in price with total world staple production, much of which is within the control of the same parent companies. In this regard these industries differ from the tariff-protected secondary manufacturers producing for a domestic market. Therefore in export-dependent regions there are few stabilizing factors.

Domestic economic stabilization policy has, at best, a small effect in Canada. The structure of the Canadian economy determines that what independent influence is possible is confined primarily to the industrial heartland of Central Canada, along the St. Lawrence River. Hinterland regions, on the other hand, are beyond domestic policy control. Thus historic policies, the increasing integration of the continental market, and the expansion of the multinational corporation have placed divisive strains on the Canadian nation.

Up to this point, our discussion has primarily focused on the problem of instability in resource regions. But this is just one manifestation of the regional problem. Policy-makers have been, for the most part, impotent in their attempts to remedy persistent regional disparities. One of the key reasons has been their unwillingness or inability to consider the large multinational corporation as the dominant economic institution of our time, even though this business form is not a recent arrival on the scene. Direct American investment in Canada extends well back into the nineteenth century, and even before the First World War there was serious concern about the expansion of American corporations not only in Canada, but around the world.[14] The pervasiveness of the American multinational influence, however, has increased over time, both through growth (in absolute terms and relative to domestic firms) and through increased integration of markets—a logical outcome of the revolutions in air transport, communications, and the increasing use of the commercial computer.

The multinational corporation has been the prime agency of continental integration, but it has not changed the century-old pattern of regional specialization. This specialization, and our inability to stabilize and develop the hinterland through national policies, is the crux of the present problem. It is a problem of hinterland regions throughout the world. "In the hinterland regions the working out of comparative advantage can result in a narrow and intense specialization in a single resource subsector, in effect tying the future of the region to the vicissitudes of national demand for the products of that subsector. This will set at least ultimate limits to the region's growth rates: shifts in national demand patterns, the emergence of substitutes, depletion, technological advances, or the relative shifting of regional advantage may at any time choke off growth and leave behind enclaves of unemployed resources and economic stagnation."[15] These effects are multiplied when the region becomes subsidiary to international demand under the hegemony of the multinationals.

There are significant obstacles in the way of solving regional inequity. Canada's regions, as mentioned before, are in fact regions of the American economy, but naturally they have no say or influence in the making of U.S. policies. In addition, regions (or provinces) with the same resources compete with each other for international capital via reduced taxation, subsidies, publicly financed infrastructure (schools, hospitals, roads, waterworks, etc.), and government loans. This tends to limit the region's (or province's) options in attempting to diversify the economic base.[16] The status quo, therefore, merely perpetuates the movement that Gunnar Myrdal has called the drift towards regional inequalities through a process of cumulative causation.[17]

Myrdal's concept contradicts the usual interpretation of orthodox economists, many of whom argue that regional inequalities tend to diminish as a result of market pressures. Their argument is that the rise in unemployment in a region depresses wages in that region and thus attracts new investment to take advantage of these lower wages. Even in the absence of factors such as market control by a few corporations, multinational firms, discriminatory freight rates, and other institutional rigidities in the contemporary North American economy, however, the dynamics of the economy preclude such an equilibrating process. As Myrdal argues, the initial decline in employment reduces regional income. This reduction is multiplied as consumer demand falls, reducing income for other industries serving the regional economy. In the face of reduced tax revenues local governments must either increase taxes or reduce services.

Either course will reduce the attractiveness of the region to investors. They, in any case, are more interested in the size of the local consumer market, favourable government subsidies, reduced taxes, and the availability of natural resources and specialized or skilled labour. Thus, the tax burden must fall either on the remaining industries or on the population. This promotes more shutdowns, an exodus of skilled labour, and a further diminution of the regional market. The disparities between regions increase rather than diminish. Such is the process that appears to have occurred in the Maritimes during this century.

The economic dominance of the multinational corporation poses specific problems quite apart from regional specialization and integration difficulties. One example of their unfavourable regional effects has been the location of most manufacturing subsidiaries in the southern Ontario region. D. M. Ray has shown that proximity to American headquarters rather than any economic factor is the reason for this concentration.[18] Firms do not move to hinterland regions unless there are very pressing reasons to do so, and no Canadian government has been willing to introduce a policy that would discriminate against the most populated region of the country. The hinterland provinces do not have the resources to compete against Ontario in the game of attempting to entice, through subsidies and tax reductions, multinational companies to locate in their provinces. More simply, decisions taken by multinational corporations are largely based on internal criteria. Traditionally it has been believed that these decisions could be influenced by national fiscal and monetary policy levers, but if this were ever true it is true no longer. In fact, few capitalist countries have had much success with regional economic development policies and Canada is no exception. The most significant result of this lack of success has been the type of economic disparities indicated in Table 1. These disparities create immense strains on the political bonds of the country, and there is no indication of a decline in the imbalances. What is to be done; what, indeed, can be done?

There has yet to develop in Canada a policy response to these disparities. Some of the responsibility for this must rest

Table 1 Regional Indicators
(Ontario = 100)

Region	Unemployment Index 1973	Average Weekly Earnings 1973	Personal Income Per Person 1971
Atlantic Provinces	222.5	82.8	61.6
Quebec	185.0	92.5	76.3
Ontario	100.0	100.0	100.0
Prairies	97.5	92.1	78.9
British Columbia	162.5	107.6	93.7
Canada	140.0	96.7	85.8

with the belief, widely held among all our political parties, that the nationality of capital ownership is unimportant—capital is capital. This is true only if one rejects the advisability or desirability of real national policies and accepts that nations should become mere regions within a larger economy.[19]

In the boom years of the 1960s, when Canada identified with the internationalist proclivities of Prime Minister Lester B. Pearson, the plan for an international agency to harmonize policy, foster development, and establish some mechanism for controlling international business came forward.[20] Nevertheless, the possibilities of concerted action appear almost non-existent. No major country has yet been willing to voluntarily concede control over its economic policy to an international agency except under a limited mandate which permits the country to withdraw if the policy of the agency conflicts with domestic priorities. The existence of a policy makes necessary a political, discretionary body to make policy. In the world of superpowers, political and discretionary power at the international level means policy control by the superpowers in their interest. It is difficult enough to press the case for the poorer regions of Canada in Ottawa, but consider the diminished magnitude of such problems in a world perspective. It would be almost impossible to find remedial measures acceptable to the regions or nations that benefit from the exploitation of the hinterland.

In any case, international agreements depend on the cooperation of *all* major nations—an unlikely prospect in the contemporary world.

Another strategy, which may be identified with the more conservative school of economists, would have Canada move towards freer trade even if only on a continental basis.[21] In an appeal to traditional economic theory, this school attacks the protective tariff system which originated with the National Policy. This alternative must be based on the thesis that Canada is not an appropriate economic policy unit and that international economic forces will produce a higher standard of living for Canadians in all regions than is presently enjoyed. There are two objections to this strategy. Not least is the political abrogation of responsibility for the state of the national economy. On a more theoretical plane, the world economy no longer exhibits, if it ever did, the characteristics on which the free trade argument is based.[22]

Since the late 1950s there has emerged a new approach with roots in the old National Policy. For lack of a better term, it may be called a second (or third?) national policy.[23] Though there is no close community of views as to what shape the new strategy should take, most would accept the aim as "to transform the regions of Canada in the second half of the twentieth century into a political and economic unit." It is clear that any such policy must begin with a recognition of the reality of the multinational corporation as the dominant international economic institution. It follows from the above analysis that the mechanism of the global firm undermines Keynesian monetary and fiscal policies at the national level through the methods elaborated above.[24] The structure of the multinational not only undermines domestic policies, it gives these firms a decided advantage over national corporations. In addition, the multinationals concentrate their branch plants in Central Canada. In other words, the increasing dominance of the branch plant can only widen the gap between metropolis and hinterland. In relative terms, the hinterland regions are "undeveloping." This continuing and increasing metropolitan dominance (Levitt has called it the evolution of the old mercantilism to the new) [25] has been a fact of life for some time.

The old mercantilism spread its imperialism through control

of the movement of goods, protecting the trade and commerce of its empire for the monopoly benefit of merchant capitalists in the metropolis. Transition to industrial capitalism was made possible by the protected markets of a hinterland. Britain, for instance, only converted to free trade *after* its dominance in world manufacturing was so well established as to preclude effective competition for almost half a century. The United States nurtured its industry on the relatively large protected continental market that was continually added to by geographic, political, and economic expansion.

Far from being a great innovation, the National Policy of John A. Macdonald was an attempt to emulate the mercantilism that had proven so successful in the American republic. But, while the three-pillared National Policy of tariff protection, transcontinental railway construction, and western settlement was successful in creating a hinterland for the commercial capital of Central Canada, it did so only after American industrial capital had already evolved, through trust, merger, and profit reinvestment, into the corporate form now described as "monopoly capitalism." De facto cartelization in the United States provided pools of capital in search of a profitable, but controlled, outlet. The protective tariffs of Canada guaranteed such a profitable investment frontier. The multinational presence in Canada, therefore, is as old as the national economy itself. The importation of goods was merely replaced by an inflow of capital and, with it, of American technology.

This inflow was superimposed on the small Canadian market. The result has been a "miniature replica" effect where corporate structure parallels that of the United States, with the addition of a few Canadian firms. The combination of the relatively small Canadian market and the capital-intensive, mass-production technology of the American corporation has produced a plethora of underutilized, and thereby inefficient, branch plants. In the face of this excess capacity it is not surprising that the financially weaker Canadian firms succumb to the invasion, finding it more profitable to sell out and become subsidiaries, than to withstand the competition—a process which has continued with increased frequency to the present.[26]

The implications of all this for the future development of industry in the less-favoured regions are important. Despite continuing high levels of tariff protection in Canada, excess manufacturing capacity already in place presents, as it has in the past, a formidable barrier to the industrialization of any of the hinterland regions and, indeed, has contributed to the stagnation of the regions already partially industrialized.[27] In fact, recent studies suggest that the branch-plant relationship contributes to a deindustrialization of Central Canada when American policy turns protectionist. Such a result is quite compatible with, if not the result of, the economic integration of Canada as a series of regions into the continental economy.

As a result of these developments, a new national policy must satisfy at least three conditions if domestic monetary and fiscal policy is to be made effective, regional imbalance rectified, and a national industrial strategy created. First, Canadian priorities must determine the regional allocation of capital. This will mean a policy to regulate the inflow and location of new capital as well as the outflow of profits, dividends, and other payments generated by existing foreign investment. In other words, the mechanisms by which multinational corporations evade national policies must be recognized and regulated.

The second imperative of a new national policy is that there must be an end to the "free" inflow of technology. This technology has often been inappropriate to the size and structure of the Canadian market, since Canada has a much smaller market and different climate than the U.S. or Europe, and has prevailed only because of Canada's tariffs. On the other hand the development of Canadian technology has been seriously hindered by the structure of the metropolis-hinterland relationship, which tends to concentrate innovative activities at the centre. The failure to develop domestic technical innovation has been repeatedly documented in Canada. A recent study by the Science Council has demonstrated the connection between the extremely low level of technological innovation in Canada and the branch-plant economy. The cause has been the importation of technology with the rise of the subsidiary. As James Laxer has argued, "companies engaged in end-product manufacturing and companies which produce parts and components often establish interconnected research communities which operate in the field of product innovation. The process cannot develop in a branch-plant economy where would-be local suppliers have to compete with foreign firms with several years lead time in producing parts and components for new end-products."[28] He also argues that the fact that fewer than 10 per cent of the scientists and engineers graduated in Canada between 1969 and 1971 got jobs in manufacturing, a precipitous decline from the early sixties, is indicative of the stagnation of domestic innovation.[29]

Whether our dependence on branch plants caused us to import technology or vice versa is a fruitless question because imported technology is embodied in the branch plant.[30] Breaking out of the cycle of dependency we will run up against major obstacles, but failing to break out will forever inhibit the expansion of Canadian manufacturing. This limitation will undercut the effectiveness of any regional development policy which could be politically feasible only if it could concentrate on new manufacturing plants, rather than the relocation of existing firms or plants. This dismal conclusion proceeds directly from Canada's current position. We rely on imported technology in a limited domestic market. We are constrained from rationalization by the branch-plant structure and the pressures of American law and we are restrained from competing in the U.S. or in other markets by the global strategies of American-backed multinationals. We are further inhibited by higher costs resulting from the inappropriateness of some mass production technologies in our small and fragmented domestic market. All these factors bar extensive development of secondary and tertiary industries, the development of a native technology, and the employment of Canadian-trained scientists and engineers.[31]

The third imperative of a new national policy is that the strategy must revolve around Canada's centres of economic strength—that is, her natural resources. In a sense this is a link with the first National Policy, a strategy based on a resource frontier. But this is not an appeal for increased exploitation of the hinterland and regions by a rapacious satellite metropolis in Central Canada, with the consequent flow of surplus value, rents, and profits to the centre from the periphery as was the ultimate result of the earlier policy. Rather, the economic surplus must remain in the periphery to be invested in economic activities that will create stable employment opportunities and decrease regional disparities. It should be remembered that, while Canada is one of the world's greatest producers of a wide range of natural products, it is still a net importer of most of the finished goods made from these same natural products,[32] even though the Canadian and potential export markets are sufficiently large to provide the necessary economies of scale for efficient production.

As long as Canadian resources are exploited by multinational corporations, which establish the subsidiaries to export Canadian raw products to supply the American industrial system, the potential growth of secondary and tertiary economic activities will not occur. Of course, American economic policy reinforces the pressures not to develop secondary industries in Canada by such measures as tariffs which place progressively higher rates on imports as the degree of manufacture increases. There also are tax incentive schemes such as the Domestic International Sales Corporation program which gives tax benefits to those multinationals that shift production from abroad to the United States and then re-export the output.

The lack of higher-order production might not be too serious if economic rents and tax revenues remained in Canada and were reinvested in the development of the resource regions.[33] But, as Eric Kierans has repeatedly demonstrated, Canada and its provinces usually receive only a miniscule fraction of the proceeds of resource extraction through taxation, royalties, and the sale of resource rights.[34] The C.P.R. was able to realize large profits out of the land resources granted it by the government; but at least much of this was reinvested, both in the railway itself and in other areas. Given the dominant control by non-Canadian companies of the contemporary natural-resource frontier, there is little hope for even this benefit from the profits these firms make.

From the above discussion emerge the imperatives of any new Canadian strategy to weld her diverse economic regions into a political-economic unit, a necessary step for dealing with regional disparities and reducing the dependence of the various regions on the U.S. economy and its policies. As in the earlier national policy, there are three critical and interrelated components of a new policy: controls on the movement of capital in terms of magnitude, direction, location, and form; a major and systematic investment in the development of business institutions, industrial techniques, and technologies suitable for the Canadian market; and a radical change in the role and mode of the exploitation of resources and energy. Also, like the old national policy, the new must be dependent upon the initiative or entrepreneurship of the state. Canadian capitalism has always been too small or too timid (or both) to take on projects for national economic integration. Evidence to this effect abounds in the histories of the St. Lawrence Seaway, from the original canals onwards, the Grand Trunk Railways and the C.P.R., Air Canada and the C.B.C. It is the tradition of Canada, largely due to economic necessity, that government, operating through both private and public institutions, has been the foremost native entrepreneur.

Since this is an important, and possibly controversial, element in the development strategy, I shall develop the argument in more detail, drawing once again from the historic role of government in Canadian economic policy. In the nineteenth century, the government was a financial intermediary—a body which operated to generate sufficient confidence in the potential of the Canadian economy to attract lenders and to provide an institutional mechanism for pooling capital to finance the massive investment in transportation facilities necessary to knit the regions of British North America into a national economy. Alfred Dubuc states that "in economic terms Confederation was essentially an instrument of public finance whose object it was to make available to those responsible for effecting investment, the resources necessary for the unified economic development of British North America."[35] At this point, transportation was the only large-scale enterprise, but its demand for capital was beyond the capability of domestic private enterprise to finance.

What was true of the nineteenth century remains true in the twentieth. Government, provincial and national, has remained the major domestic financial intermediary on most of the large-scale, capital-intensive, new developments not accounted for by the expansion of the multinationals. Equally significant with governments' entrepreneurial role in developing transportation and communications has been its participation in energy production, with Atomic Energy of Canada at the national level and the publicly owned hydroelectric companies at the provincial. It is significant that British Columbia, Quebec, and Newfoundland have quite recently taken over privately owned utilities because these private firms were unable or unwilling to invest in the expansion desired by the provincial authorities.

To cast the debate in more theoretical terms we can agree with John Kenneth Galbraith that the nature of modern industry, modern technology, and contemporary market structure is such that the risks and the capital requirements are so great that anybody entering industry must have such enormous capital resources and diversity of income sources that the risk of failure or even of delayed returns in any one endeavour will not threaten the collapse of the whole company.[36] Yet it is possible to think of only a few Canadian corporations other than the government which can take such risks. Thus, if the government is precluded by ideological considerations from taking the role of entrepreneur, the job, by default, must fall to the multinationals. This will eliminate the opportunity to devise a national policy and, in turn, perpetuate the problems of regional imbalance, instability, and disintegration.

In the resource field, Eric Kierans has advanced the proposition that the public presence should be concentrated at the primary production stage, on the grounds that the profits from the exploitation of natural resources should accrue to the ultimate owners, the Canadian public.[37] While one can hardly disagree with the logic of his position, it has a major weakness as a total resource strategy. Much of the wealth may be at the primary production stage, but the expansion of economic and employment opportunities in the hinterland regions is determined by the development of secondary processing and manufacturing. As long as this latter stage of development is determined by the global strategies of the international companies, heavily influenced by policies in other countries, the whole question of regional development policy in Canada must remain in abeyance.

Recently some provinces, particularly in Western Canada, have instituted royalty policies designed to return a higher percentage of resource revenues to provincial coffers with the expressed goal of providing investment funds to establish industries that would diversify the provincial economic base or provide alternatives for exhaustible resources. It is ironic that after years of disregard for the regional problem, the national government has attempted, through corporate income tax policy, to prevent the provinces from pursuing such a policy, on the grounds that the whole nation should benefit from the bounties of nature. Such an eleventh-hour conversion would be more convincing if this concern was translated into any discernable regional development policy which would attempt to distribute industrial activity on a more balanced basis across the country, in exchange for pooling and redistributing resource income from the hinterland to the metropolis. What cannot be overemphasized is that economic development in the resource regions requires a commitment from the superior economic authority to pursue this goal which, in the Canadian context, implies a two-stage process—the reestablishment of the national authority as the agency of economic control and its commitment to the goal of equitable regional development.

It has been economic orthodoxy to oppose national policies because of the protectionism inherent in them. Traditionally it is argued that protectionism raises the cost of manufactured goods resulting in economic inefficiency in the allocation of resources. At best, it is allowed, protectionism in Canada has increased the country's population at the expense of a reduced per-capita income.[38] In contemporary terms, however, the traditional protectionist, like the traditional free trader, is not so much wrong as irrelevant in terms of a national strategy.

The argument that Canada is dependent on a continued inflow of American technology is less easy to dismiss. Historically, American secondary industry invaded the world because of its technical advances in mass production and mass marketing techniques. As Mira Wilkins writes, "the U.S. triumph abroad was one of ingenuity: new products, new methods of manufacturing, and new sales techniques."[39] Initial sales offices became factories to avoid the tariff and to protect patents. But this created a cycle of increased technological dependency that could only be broken by removing the institutional link that transmits the parent's technology to the subsidiary, that is, the branch-plant organization. This is because the multinationals centre research at the parent. As a result, Canada has the most dismal record of research and development expenditures of all developed Western countries.[40] Failure to develop technology appropriate to Canada inhibits the development of secondary industry and export potential. This, in turn, condemns industry to branch plants serving the domestic market, with higher level activities, including research and development, centred at the parent. The circle is complete. Already a very high percentage of Canadian research and development is initiated and financed by government or by Crown corporations like Atomic Energy of Canada and Polymer. It appears obvious that further change is unlikely to occur without substantial state impetus. Canada cannot develop all of its own technology. This should not lead, however, as it so often does, to the assumption that the domination of the multinational corporation is a necessary price to pay for technology. As Rutenberg points out, "technology that is almost as efficient is available as turn-key plants from specialized construction companies, or from licensors."[41] Turn-key plants are those ready to begin production "at the turn of a key." Canada could gain considerable freedom and flexibility by purchasing unmodified American technology which accompanies the establishment of multinational subsidiaries in this country.

In economic policy-making, Canada is faced with persistent problems of regional imbalance and distress which have contributed to severe regional alienation as well as to national problems of unemployment and inflation. The ensuing national debate over the whole range of stabilization, growth, and regional economic balance policies has assumed that the Canadian economy is an appropriate policy-making unit. The evidence, however, points to the conclusion that, in the present institutional framework, it is not. Rather, Canada should be considered as a group of regions within the larger North American economy.

The Canadian dilemma in this context is obvious. The regional problems which are straining the bonds of Confederation but which are integral to the economic structure of the nation since its creation, are insoluble with the policy tools available. They are insoluble because of the emergence of the multinational corporation and the concomitant free flow of capital which effectively neutralizes the traditional levers of economic policy. The realistic alternatives facing Canada, therefore, are either to accede to the continental, integrative pressures of the multinational corporations or to work towards a new national policy that is based on contemporary economic realities and not on nineteenth-century protectionism.

The crux of the regional problem is the allocation of capital investment. In Canada the provinces do not have the tools, nor has the federal government the will, to effect any marked change from the pattern now determined by the global companies. What then can be said of regional input into shaping new policies? Existing political mechanisms appear ill suited to ensure hinterland participation. With the exception of the brief and unsuccessful Diefenbaker interlude, the domination of the major national political parties by Central Canada precludes any effective restructuring of national and regional policy even if appropriate policies could be devised and accepted.

The main potential for regional input appears to lie with the provinces which possess natural resources required by the metropolis region. It was the need for oil that finally prompted some federal accommodation towards the West in 1973. The Atlantic region does not have that resource lever. At the same time, as already noted, the federal government has attempted to block the mineral-rich provinces from using the tool of resource royalties to develop the hinterland regions industrially by providing that provincial royalties not be deductible for income tax purposes. Thus, the federal government would emasculate one of the few provincial levers in economic development, although there is little indication that the provinces have contemplated the economic ramifications on projected development policies of the existing control of mineral production by the multinational corporations.

Paradoxically, perhaps, the only potential solution lies in a reaffirmation of federal authority over the national economy and regional investment priorities, thereby superceding the existing control of the global corporations. In short, it means recognizing present-day realities, looking at the mechanisms and institutions of continental integration. Capital and technology flow within the multinationals. Any alternative must include the controlling of direct capital flows and that means the development of new capital sources and new investment opportunities in the domestic resource frontier, under Canadian control and direction. It also means developing technology and market structures tailored to Canadian domestic and export needs. Regional input must come as continual political pressure on the national government to move in the direction of a new policy.

The major break, not with the real past, but with an ideological mystification of the past, should be the reestablishment of the central role of the government. Canadian private enterprise has neither the size and diversity, nor the inclination, to absorb the risks, since it has always found it more profitable to act as a commercial agent for larger foreign capital aggregations than risk independent entrepreneurship. The alternative to government initiative, therefore, is increasing reliance on the large international companies whose global orientation can only exacerbate the internal policy problems of the Canadian nation. As Papandreou has made very explicit, "the multinational corporation, more than any other institutional development in the West, makes mandatory a bold departure toward *political economy.*"[42] Only if we recognize that the multinational corporations affect the very structure and operation of the Canadian economy can we develop the measures that will return political control of the economy to Canada and make the country an economic unit "worth talking about."

NOTES

1. A.M.C. Waterman, "The Canadian Fallacy" (paper presented to the Seventh Annual Meeting of the Canadian Economics Association, Kingston, June 1973).
2. Ibid., p. 18.
3. V.C. Fowke, *The National Policy and the Wheat Economy* (Toronto, 1957), p. 8; emphasis added.
4. Ibid. For a more recent interpretation along the same lines, see R.T. Naylor, "The Rise and Fall of the Third Commercial Empire of the St. Lawrence," in *Capitalism and the National Question in Canada,* ed. Gary Teeple (Toronto, 1972).
5. V.C. Fowke and G.E. Britnell, *An Historical Analysis of the Crow's Nest Pass Agreement and Grain Rates: A Study in National Transportation Policy* (a submission of the province of Saskatchewan to the Royal Commission on Transportation, 1960).
6. Canada, *Report* of the Royal Commission on Dominion-Provincial Relations, Book I, reprinted in *The Dirty Thirties,* ed. M. Horn, (Toronto, 1972), pp. 170, 173.
7. V.C. Fowke, "National Policy—Old and New," *Canadian Journal of Economics and Political Science* (August 1952).
8. If one were to identify a "new national policy," one would have to consider the most explicit attempt as the bilingualism and biculturalism program beginning in the 1960s. This, however, cannot be seen as an economic program of much significance to the economic vitality or viability of the hinterland.
9. David Rutenberg, "The Advantages of Being Multinational," in *The Multinational Firm and the Nation State,* ed. Gilles Paquet (Don Mills, 1972), p. 107.
10. Andreas Papandreou, "Multinational Corporations and Empire," *Social Praxis,* I (2), p. 108. See also Lawrence Copithorne, "The Static Theory of the Multinational Firm" (unpublished paper, University of Manitoba, 1972).
11. "With over 60% of both exports and imports accounted for by trade with the United States, Canada can no longer be said to carry on a multilateral, basically triangular, international trade; instead, her trade is concentrated in a bilateral way, on the United States." H.G. Johnson, *The Canadian Quandary* (Toronto, 1963), p. 97.
12. *Task Force on the Structure of Canadian Industry,* (Ottawa, 1968), p. 6.
13. See S.M. Jamieson, "Regional Factors in Industrial Conflict: The Case of British Columbia", *Canadian Journal of Economics and Political Science* (August 1962).
14. Mira Wilkins, *The Emergence of the Multinational Enterprise* (Cambridge, Mass., 1970), particularly chap. 10.
15. H. Perloff and L. Wingo, "National Resource Endowment and Regional Economic Growth," in *Regional Development and Planning,* ed. J. Friedman and W. Alonso (Cambridge, Mass., 1964), pp. 232-33.

16. Eric Kierans, "Canadian Resources Policy" (paper presented to the Seventh Annual Meeting of the Canadian Economics Association, Kingston, June 1973).
17. Gunnar Myrdal, *Rich Lands and Poor* (New York, 1957), pp. 23-38.
18. D.M. Ray, "The Spacial Structure of Regional Development and Cultural Differences: A Factorial Ecology of Canada, 1961" (paper presented to the Annual Regional Sciences Association Meeting, November 1968), pp. 15-16.
19. " ... Canada is an American nation, an integral part of the North American political and economic continent; and Canada is becoming increasingly an integral part of North America. Further, both politically and economically, the general trend of world evolution is toward regionalism, toward political and economic organization on a continental ... rather than national scale." Johnson, *The Canadian Quandary*, p. 103.
20. See for example the Economic Council of Canada, *Interim Report on Competition Policy* (Ottawa, 1969), pp. 180-81; and *Task Force on the Structure of Canadian Industry*, p. 402.
21. Johnson, *The Canadian Quandary*, particularly chap. 10.
22. The traditional neoclassic argument assumes competition in a static framework and with no positive externalities of scale. Neither of these conditions holds. Secondly, as the Myrdal model shows, market forces lead to an exacerbation of regional disequilibrium. Finally, and possibly most persuasive in real terms, the abandonment of protection in Canada and the U.S. at this time would appear politically impossible.
23. The two major schools addressing themselves to the problem are the "liberal" Committee for an Independent Canada, headed by people such as Walter Gordon, Abe Rotstein, and Mel Hurtig, and the socialist Waffle group, headed by people such as Mel Watkins, James Laxer, and Cy Gonick.
24. See J. K. Galbraith, *The New Industrial State* (New York, 1967), pp. 38-39.
25. Kari Levitt, *Silent Surrender* (Toronto, 1970), chap. 2.
26. The average annual number of foreign mergers and takeovers by quinquennial period, 1945-1971, is as follows: 1945-49, 15.2; 1950-54, 22.6; 1955-59, 52.2; 1960-64, 75.8; 1965-69, 114.8; (two years only) 1970-71, 146.5. Source: Toronto *Globe and Mail*, 3 May, 1972.
27. See Bruce Archibald, "Atlantic Region Underdevelopment and Socialism," in *Essays on the Left*, ed. Laurier LaPierre et al. (Toronto, 1971), pp. 103-20; and J. Laxer, "Canadian Manufacturing and U.S. Trade Policy," in *(Canada) Ltd.*, ed. R. Laxer (Toronto, 1973).
28. Laxer, "Canadian Manufacturing," pp. 132-33.
29. Ibid.
30. Wilkins, *Emergence of the Multinational Enterprise*, p. 214.
31. If, because of a limited labour market, Canadian-trained personnel migrate to jobs with U.S. parent companies, this constitutes the expropriation of human capital to the metropolis. The same mechanism operates within the hinterland—when trained personnel leave the Maritimes or the West to take jobs in Ontario. The process is cumulative and pyramidic.

32. Laxer, "Canadian Manufacturing," p. 131.
33. Johnson, among other economists, stresses the benefits to the host country from tax receipts. See Johnson, *The Canadian Quandary*, pp. xv-xvi.
34. Kierans, "Canadian Resources Policy," pp. 22-23; see also Kierans, *Report on Natural Resources Policy in Manitoba* (Winnipeg, 1973), chap. 4.
35. A. Dubuc, quoted by S. Ryerson, *Unequal Union* (Toronto, 1968), p. 344.
36. Galbraith, *The New Industrial State*, particularly chaps. 2 and 3.
37. Kierans, "Canadian Resources Policy."
38. J. Dales, *The Protective Tariff in Canada's Development* (Toronto, 1965).
39. Wilkins, *Emergence of the Multinational Enterprise*, p. 66.
40. Levitt, *Silent Surrender*, p. 130.
41. Rutenberg, "Advantages of Being Multinational," p. 102.
42. Papandreou, "Multinational Corporations," p. 107.

CARMAN MILLER

The Restoration of Greater Nova Scotia

In 1964, the idea of Maritime union, that Sleeping Beauty of Canadian politics, seemed to be awakening from the slumber to which the Maritime fathers of Confederation consigned it in 1864 when they endorsed the British North America plan unveiled by the Canadian delegates to the Charlottetown Conference. A hundred years later the Liberal premier of New Brunswick, Louis Robichaud, called for a reconsideration of Maritime union at the close of an uneventful re-enactment of the Charlottetown Conference. Much to everyone's surprise, Robert Stanfield, Nova Scotia's Conservative premier, responded favourably, and the two provinces created a joint provincial study committee to examine the proposal. Across the country the subject received wide and generally favourable publicity and many studies and articles appeared.[1] Writers who supported union usually tried to show that many Maritimers, before Confederation and now, considered union a more realistic course than that set out in the British North America Act because of the region's geographic, economic, and demographic composition. This article is intended to trace and bolster that argument by suggesting the artificial nature of the separate provincial boundaries of the mid-nineteenth century.

In 1864, the restoration of Greater Nova Scotia seemed more likely to happen than it had at any time since the separation of Prince Edward Island (Ile St. Jean) in 1769 and New Brunswick and Cape Breton Island in 1784.[2] Through the years the peninsula which lost the estate but retained the title never lacked an articulate advocate of restoration. At one time or another prominent public men such as J. B. Uniacke, J. W. Johnston, Charles Tupper, and Joseph Howe espoused the cause of union with varying degrees of conviction. In 1819 the Nova Scotian Assembly passed a resolution calling for the restoration of the islands of Prince Edward and Cape Breton. The recent publication of Tupper's Charlottetown Conference minutes makes it clear that the Maritime fathers of Confederation gave the subject much more serious consideration in 1864 than past historians have believed.[3] But was union in 1864 really practical? Perhaps it was simply a clever rhetorical tactic to sabotage discussion of the larger British North American proposal or, more devious still, a thinly veiled effort to wring better terms from the wily Canadian visitors.[4]

The Maritime region, of course, was far from monolithic. In 1864 it resembled nothing more than a loose confederation of sub-regions which defied existing political boundaries. By the mid-nineteenth century, Nova Scotia, probably the most self-conscious political entity, consisted of a rough patch-work of ethnic communities hugging a 4,625-mile coastline, each group occupying the general territory staked out by its migrant ancestors. The chief agents of socialization—family, school, church, and communications—remained ethnically defined. Nova Scotia's 1841 School Act, for example, authorized public funding for English, French, Gaelic, and German language schools, a stipulation upon which the Assembly insisted despite opposition from the Executive Council. Both church and school became stalwart defenders of minority languages.[5] And no institution defied these religious, regional, and ethnic cleavages with impunity, as the early Dalhousie College learned. Created as a non-denominational provincial university to reduce the proliferation of sectarian institutions demanding provincial aid, Dalhousie was, in the words of one of its historians, "an idea prematurely born into an alien and unfriendly world, deserted by its parents, betrayed by its guardians, and throughout its minority abused by its friends and enemies alike."[6] The controversial college system was but an institutional expression of the province's regional, religious, and ethnic diversity.

These ethnic communities suffered few collective identity crises. The Lunenburg "Dutch," recruited a century before from the Palatinate and Upper Rhine, the New England Planters, Loyalist or stolid Cumberland Yorkshiremen, not to mention the Indians, Blacks, Acadians, Protestant Pictou Scots, and Cape Breton Highlanders needed no one to tell them who they were; they had been born that way and had every intention of remaining that way. The "Nova Scotianess" of Nova Scotia, despite the coaxings of men like Joseph Howe, remained a somewhat elusive quality confined largely to a handful of self-conscious well-wishers in and around the provincial capital. Indeed Howe's own peculiar political success as the "Voice of Nova Scotia"[7] was based on his practical recognition of, and his efforts to consolidate and articulate, the province's regional diversity which he understood so well. The regions, it is true, might unite for specific political action. Pictou radicals and New England democrats might join hands to assault the political, economic, or religious privilege of Halifax but there was no fusion. To a Cape Breton Highland Scot, even a Protestant one, a Nova Scotian was, in the words of a perceptive historical novelist, "not like ourselves ... the Nova Scotians were like the Lowlanders, English, Dutch, French and every trash."[8]

No Nova Scotian lived more than thirty-five miles from the sea. And the sea, the most formative influence on Maritime development,[9] divided the province. The sea's abundance and easy access drew men from the land. Land communications, particularly roads, developed slowly. In this era no recognized provincial metropolitan centre arose, save perhaps for Boston, which must have seemed more real to most Nova Scotians outside the provincial capital than Halifax. Perhaps more Nova Scotians first met in Boston than in any provincial centre. No more eloquent testimony exists to the historic strength of Nova Scotia's ethno-regional demographic composition than the persistence of distinctive regional accents within the province into the twentieth century.

But while the sea divided the province, it also carved out

more natural subregions within the Maritime area. The Bay of Fundy and the Northumberland Strait provide two of the most obvious examples. Although far from homogeneous or self-contained, these subregions contained some striking similarities and developed a community of interests which often erased existing political boundaries. The Fundy formed the heartland of what has been called New England's Outpost[10] or Nova Scotia's Massachusetts.[11] Even in French colonial times this Baie Française had been a commercial adjunct of Massachusetts.[12] The expulsion of the Acadians and the subsequent influx of New England Planters and, later, Loyalists, stamped the area with an American character, which even large-scale early nineteenth-century British immigration failed to erase. Initial differences may have divided Loyalist from pre-Loyalist as they squabbled over the meagre crumbs of available provincial patronage, but they soon resolved these differences and lived together peacefully, the quintessence of His Majesty's Yankees.[13]

Creed constituted a second important bond in the Fundy community. Here the strength of Baptists and Methodists and the relative weakness of Catholics, Presbyterians, and Anglicans emphasized the area's non-conformist American character. For example, 60 per cent of Nova Scotia's 55,336 Baptists, the province's third largest religious denomination, resided in the Fundy-bordered counties of Cumberland, Colchester, Hants, Kings, Annapolis, and Digby.[14] In Kings and Annapolis counties they constituted the single largest religious group and represented over half the population. Across the Fundy, on the New Brunswick side, the Baptists, that province's largest Protestant denomination, possessed comparable strength, particularly in the counties of Charlotte, Albert, and Westmorland. In Charlotte and Westmorland, Baptists accounted for 22 and 27 per cent, respectively, of the population, while in Albert they comprised as much as 61 per cent. In contrast, Catholicism, both provinces' largest religious body, remained extremely weak in the Fundy area, outside of Westmorland and Saint John city and county. For example, only 12 per cent of Nova Scotia's 86,281 Catholics resided in the Fundy counties. Similarly Presbyterianism, Nova Scotia's largest Protestant denomination, languished on both sides of the Fundy, save for the counties of

Hants, Colchester, and Cumberland. (But both Cumberland and Colchester, it should be remembered, possessed another Maritime front, the Northumberland Strait, which was, as we shall see, "old country" in origin and religion.)

In an era when the church touched many more facets of men's lives than it does today, religion provided important social linkages. Through the exchange of clergy, religious gatherings, church meetings, literature, education, and the press, a region with a high degree of religious affinity found a community of interests and a common sense of purpose. No better example of the pervasive power of religion, and its ability to shape the mind of a people, can be found than the Henry Alline revival which swept this area during the revolt in the American colonies, a revival which gave these recently uprooted peoples a new sense of regional identity.[15]

The sea provided an open invitation to commerce and communication. Across the generally placid bay, men and material moved with relative ease. As early as 1770, a ferry service "of sorts"[16] plied the forty-five-mile stretch of water which separated Saint John from Annapolis Basin. At the same time smaller and often larger craft sailed between Windsor, Parrsboro, Lower Horton, Londonderry, Annapolis, Digby, Saint John, and St. Martin's. By 1836, when the only regular, official communication between Halifax and Annapolis consisted of a weekly, subsidized stage-coach service, which cost ten dollars one way and took two days, Saint John ran a regular, weekly, subsidized steamship service to both Annapolis and Windsor, which took six to eight hours and cost $1.50.[17] Nor did the line seem to suffer when a private, unsubsidized Nova Scotia concern, the Annapolis County Steamship Company, began competitive operations that same year. By 1849, the Annapolis–Digby–Windsor–Saint John line had increased its operations to bi-weekly services. In these circumstances Halifax's economic control over the area was severely compromised.

In the Fundy, Saint John's size and proximity gave it a marked advantage over Halifax. Nova Scotia's Fundy farmers and fishermen found the New Brunswick centre a much more natural market than their own provincial capital. With a population larger than Halifax, Saint John was the third largest city in British North America and controlled the lucrative timber trade of the Saint John Valley. New Brunswick's notorious neglect of agriculture during the high days of the timber trade, together with Saint John's location in a county with a low percentage of arable land, made that city an absorbent market for Nova Scotia's Fundy farmers. New Brunswick's importation of the principal crops of these farmers (cattle, horses, hogs, fruit, and potatoes) helped create a volume of trade with Nova Scotia surpassed only by that of the United Kingdom and the United States. It is probably no coincidence, therefore, that the potato was king in the Annapolis Valley when New Brunswick was "one vast lumber camp."[18] The great New Brunswick potato culture arose later on the depleted timber lands. In 1861, for example, Kings County, Nova Scotia's most productive potato-growing area, alone produced 858,551 bushels of potatoes, equivalent to one-fifth of New Brunswick's total potato crop. This huge Kings County crop probably found a ready market across the bay in the New Brunswick lumber camps as food for the Irish lumberjacks. Thus Nova Scotia's Fundy farmers shared New Brunswick's prosperity and doubtless felt the first effects of its recession.

Nova Scotia's Fundy fishermen also found their way to Saint John despite the protests of envious Halifax merchants. Apart from its proximity, Saint John's free-port status, its control of solar salt, its higher fish bounties and lower duties on imported goods made it a logical market and outfitting port.[19] Here fishermen brought their catch, outfitted their vessels, and purchased winter supplies. Here they also transported agricultural products and gypsum, the latter a very lucrative colonial trade item brought to Saint John or St. Andrews for transshipment to the United States.[20] Saint John not only was a well-stocked entrepot but possessed a good range of native manufactures: nail, tack, boot, shoe, cotton, and paper factories, as well as tanneries and foundries. Halifax merchants and government officials, conscious of their loss of trade and public revenue, attempted to break this thriving Saint John axis. Yet despite the imposition of higher duties on products purchased in New Brunswick, the proliferation of custom officials, the concession of warehouse facilities to certain Fundy ports, the construction of the abortive Shubenacadie Canal, and the launching of a Halifax–Fundy steam service, their efforts seem to have reaped only limited success by mid-century.[21] So they turned to rails. By 1859 forty-five miles of track connected Halifax to the closest Fundy port, Windsor. This was the first leg of a railway, the Windsor–Annapolis, which would bring the Fundy counties of Hants, Kings, Annapolis, and Digby under closer commercial supervision. But by Confederation Halifax's battle appeared to have been far from successful. "The facilities afforded for the constant interchange of commodities between Saint John and the western parts of Nova Scotia," *The McAlpine's Maritime Directory* boasted in 1870, " . . . (have) created a large trade in the articles manufactured in St. John."

Shipbuilding flourished on both sides of the Fundy and reached fever proportions during the "Golden" decades of the 1850s and the 1860s. Stimulated by the Australia and California gold rushes, immigration, and two external wars, the Crimean and the American Civil wars, this industry grew to great proportions and enriched many an enterprising businessman. It also formed the base of the region's lucrative carrying trade. Saint John became the "closest approximation to a centre for the industry." There and across the bay in small ports like Digby, Kingsport, Maitland, Windsor, and Parrsboro, to name only a few, were built some of the largest and best square-rigged vessels in the world. And "by the 1850s the combined operation of the three Maritime Colonies was sufficient to rank them fourth behind Great Britain, France and the United States among the sailing nations of the world."[22] In this world of wind, water, and sail the Fundy held a pivotal place. In 1861, for example, Nova Scotia's Fundy counties accounted for 77 (or 36 per cent) of all the province's vessels launched and 46 per cent (12,233 tons) of its tonnage.

Not surprisingly, Nova Scotia's Fundy counties, particularly Kings and Cumberland, registered the most striking population increases in the province between 1851 and 1861. Some of the newcomers came from across the Bay. Indeed, 74 per cent (1,673) of all immigrants born in New Brunswick and living in Nova Scotia in 1861 had settled in the six Fundy counties. Eleven per cent (258) of the rest went to Halifax city. Moreover, prosperity muted any potentially divisive effects of trade rivalry. Shipbuilding ports like Windsor could scarcely keep pace with demands and frequently placed orders for vessels in New Brunswick, particularly St. Martin's.[23] Similarly, many vessels registered in Saint John were built in Nova Scotia. In 1854, for example, 80 per cent of the tonnage built in Digby county yards, one of the largest shipbuilding counties in the province, went to colonial ports, "presumably New Brunswick."[24] Sails and other building materials came from Saint John. Altogether then, the Fundy Basin, in the decades preceding Confederation, seemed to constitute an open-ended community based on ethnic, religious, and commercial ties which transgressed existing political boundaries.

A similar pattern emerged in the Northumberland Strait area. There the interests of three provincial territories converged within the larger economy of the Gulf of St. Lawrence, whose borders extended as far as Quebec and included the Baie des Chaleurs, Ile Magdalen, and Newfoundland. The Nova Scotia counties of Inverness, Antigonish, Pictou, Colchester, and Cumberland, together with the New Brunswick counties of Westmorland and Kent, formed the southern borders of the Northumberland Strait, which was bounded on the north by Prince Edward Island. Settled largely by old-country immigrants of French, Scottish, Irish, and Yorkshire descent, the Northumberland, like the Fundy, formed a community based on culture and commerce.

Although a high degree of religious homogeneity characterized the Northumberland Strait area, the original ethno-religious pattern of settlement remained clearly discernable almost a hundred years later. Nearly a century after the arrival of the good ship *Hector,* that tired, rotten old boat which brought New Scotland its first sizable consignment of Scots, 84 per cent of Pictou County's population was Presbyterian. On Pictou's eastern border—the location to which the stern Pictou Protestant divines reputedly directed a shipload of their fellow Highlanders who were of the Catholic persuasion—Antigonish County remained 83 per cent Roman Catholic. Yorkshire Methodism still thrived in Colchester, Cumberland, and Westmorland. On the other hand, the Baptists, the dominant religion of the Fundy, constituted an insignificant force outside the two-fronted Fundy–Northumberland counties of Colchester, Cumberland, and Westmorland, a numerical weakness matched only by the Church of England. Presbyterians were as dominant in the Northumberland Strait area as were Baptists in the Fundy, and Catholics were the next most numerous group. Obviously this area, with all respect to the perceptions of Sam Slick, possessed more than "a cross of the Scotch."[25]

Ecclesiastical administration reinforced regional religious bonds. The jurisdiction of the Bishop of the Church of England in Nova Scotia included the small Anglican community on Prince Edward Island. Until 1868 the island's Baptists formed part of the small Eastern Baptist Association of Nova Scotia. Similar arrangements existed for the major denominations in the Strait. The Roman Catholic Diocese of Charlottetown, separated from Quebec in 1829, included Ile Magdalen and New Brunswick and, for all practical purposes, eastern Nova Scotia and Cape Breton until the creation of the Arichat Diocese in 1844. By mid-century the Synod of the Presbyterian Church of Nova Scotia, the province's largest Presbyterian faction, consisted of four presbyteries: Pictou, Truro, Prince Edward Island, and Halifax. Their closest Presbyterian rival, the Church of Scotland, maintained a similar structural arrangement, except that it had a presbytery at Cape Breton instead of one at Truro.

The ease of water communications within the Strait gave these arrangements validity. Only fourteen miles separated Pictou County (Caribou) from Prince Edward Island (Wood Island). Less than nine miles lay between the island and New Brunswick (Cape Tormentine). And both were navigable for at least eight months of the year. As early as 1775 Prince Edward Island's lieutenant-governor, Walter Patterson, who owned large tracts of land in Pictou County which he wished to sell, recognized the importance of continuous communication with Nova Scotia and attempted to establish a regular summer service between Wood Island and Pictou. By 1825, an island-subsidized packet made weekly voyages to Pictou to complement the more irregular, privately operated, ferry service which had been established as early as 1807. Meanwhile a freight and passenger schooner service ran between Pictou and the Miramichi and competed with a Halifax-based steamship line plying between Halifax, Arichat, Pictou, Charlottetown, the Miramichi, and Percé. Regular triangular sea communications between Nova Scotia, New Brunswick, and Prince Edward Island were completed in 1836 when the New Brunswick Legislature, under pressure from "gentlemen in the Northumberland Strait area"[26] offered a sizable subsidy for regular steamboat service between the Miramichi, Charlottetown, and Pictou. The official intercolonial postal route, which ran a tri-weekly summer service, Pictou–Shediac–Charlottetown–Pictou, accentuated these triangular lines. The steamer *John McAdam* which serviced this route had an eighty-passenger capacity, fifty first class and thirty in the cabins. Soon an elaborate network of steam and sail boats connected Cape Breton, Pictou, Prince Edward Island, northern New Brunswick, and the Gulf of St. Lawrence.

Along these sea lanes, ideas, men, and material moved with relative facility. Newspapers like Pictou's *Colonial Standard* commanded an extensive circulation in eastern Nova Scotia and Cape Breton. According to the 1861 census 54 per cent (471) of all immigrants to Nova Scotia born in Prince Edward Island settled in the five Northumberland Strait counties of Cumberland, Colchester, Pictou, Antigonish, and Inverness. The city of Halifax absorbed 13 per cent (117) while the Atlantic coast counties of Cape Breton Island, that is Richmond and Cape Breton counties, which were so easily accessible through the Canso Strait and Loch Bras D'Or, claimed another 16 per cent (138). In the absence of precise inter-regional trade statistics, the volume and nature of commerce can only be inferred. Moreover as T. C. Haliburton warned readers in 1829, Nova Scotia's early official statistics "must be purely relative due to the very great volume and extent of illicit trade and smuggling." We know, however, that Pictou coal found an open market in Prince Edward Island, New Brunswick, and, more particularly, in the gulf and at Quebec and Montreal. Pictou also supplied "the Miramichi and other lumbering districts of New Brunswick" with pork, butter, and beef.[27] Prince Edward Island landed flour at Pictou where it was doubtlessly transshipped. Other Prince Edward Island agricultural produce—barley, turnips, potatoes, and pork—according to the *McAlpine*

Maritime Directory, found a ready market in the "Lower Provinces,"[28] probably in the lumber camps along the Miramichi, Nespisiguit, and Restigouche. In other words, food followed the seasonal migration of a portion of the island's labour force.

Even before the advent of steam, Pictou occupied a pivotal position in the economy of the Northumberland Strait, a position similar to that of Saint John in the Fundy. As early as 1830 Joseph Howe noted Pictou's brisk trade with Prince Edward Island and northern New Brunswick.[29] This was scarcely news in Halifax. Four years earlier a committee of the Halifax Commercial Society, contemplating a regular Halifax–Quebec steam service, realized they would have to break into the lucrative gulf trade to make their project successful. Pictou's command of good agricultural land, prime pine timber stands, coal, and one of the few good harbours on Nova Scotia's gulf shore gave it an enviable positional advantage. Agriculture, lumbering, shipbuilding, and mining flourished. Its early dominance of the trans-Atlantic timber trade, its solar salt supply, and its free-port status suggest that it possessed sufficient managerial skills to exploit its natural advantages. Pictou, therefore, soon became an important commercial centre, "the resort of coasters from, and the emporium of trade of, all the lower Gulf of Saint Lawrence."[30] Here vessels for the gulf cod and mackerel fisheries came to be outfitted and to dispose of their catch, ships were bought and sold, and farmers disposed of their surplus produce. An 1823 petition to the Nova Scotia legislature claimed that shrewd Pictou merchants, through their control of solar salt, had brought fishermen as far afield as the Magdalen Islands to a state of utter dependency. One of these successful early Pictou merchants, Edward Mortimer, at his death in 1819, possessed eighty vessels committed to the gulf provisioning trade.[31] In Nova Scotia by 1836 the value of Pictou's trade was surpassed only by Halifax.[32] The advent of steam simply improved Pictou's position.

Of course both the Northumberland Strait and the Fundy opened into a large economy. The Northumberland was tied as closely to a trans-Atlantic trade axis as the Fundy was tied to the American–Caribbean, though even this characterization is far from exclusive. A. G. Bailey has described colonial New

Brunswick as two provinces, one with an Atlantic frontage, the other a St. Lawrence one. "Within the two geographic provinces," he has written, "there evolved early in colonial times two competing societies, that of the St. Lawrence occupied by the British and that of the Atlantic occupied by Britain and the United States."[33] What Bailey has written of colonial New Brunswick might be said with equal validity of the pre-Confederation Maritime colonies. Both the Northumberland and the Fundy possessed definable geo-economic borders which erased existing political boundaries. Mid-century advocates of Maritime union, therefore, may have only sought more realistic, if less tidy, regional political boundaries.

The precise arguments the Maritime fathers of Confederation used at Charlottetown, for or against the restoration of Greater Nova Scotia, may never be known. But it is conceivable that a plan of regional union based on the construction of a canal through Chignecto, which would connect the Northumberland Strait to the Fundy, may have made sense to many perceptive Maritimers in 1864, either as a prelude to the larger British North American union or as an end in itself. On the other hand Halifax merchants would scarcely have welcomed a canal which would grant Saint John easier access to the gulf.[34] Moreover, equally perceptive Maritimers, foreseeing the end of the old wood, wind, and water economy, might have argued that the growth of a rail-bound land economy would not only make isolation impossible but would give validity to existing provincial political borders.[35] None seems to have predicted the effects of the growth of the state, particularly the federal state, upon regional socio-economic development. Nor did they seem to appreciate their own potential weakness once left without an effective regional political power centre. United, the Maritimes may have achieved some mastery in their own house. Divided, they were easily ruled.

The Maritime fathers of Confederation decided at Charlottetown, Canadian money and coercion did the rest, and Confederation became a fact. In vain Joseph Howe tried to short-circuit the Confederation scheme with talk of Maritime union. Even the election of a provincial government committed to separation failed to convince the federal and imperial governments. Stripped of their previous powers over currency, banking, commerce, transportation, and the major revenue sources, provincial governments increasingly became dependent upon federal largesse. George Brown of the *Globe* might make his annual editorial plea for Maritime union within the larger Confederation, but John A. Macdonald rejected this plan and could not be expected to endorse the creation of a potentially more powerful regional bloc in an area of latent disaffection.

The completion of the Intercolonial Railway in 1876 consolidated federal control over the Maritimes. Slowly it wended its leisurely course through the New Brunswick forests on its way to Halifax which federalist advocates had promised would become the Liverpool of British North America. Between Rivière du Loup and Halifax it managed to pass through "no less than fourteen constituencies."[36] At Truro it finally made contact with the Eastern Extension which ran from there to the coal pits of Pictou, one of the areas of strongest federal sympathy. Everywhere the railway went it made converts for Confederation and confirmed the faith of federalist friends.

Enterprising businessmen of Central Canada followed the steel; indeed, many had preceded it. They found the Maritime market much more lucrative than they had anticipated at the time of Confederation. The tariff, too, worked its spell, and Nova Scotian industrial output, between the years 1880 and 1890, outstripped that of both Ontario and Quebec. As T. W. Acheson has written, the Maritimes, by 1885, "provided a striking illustration of the success of that National Policy. With less than one-fifth of the population of the Dominion, the region contained eight of the twenty-three Canadian cotton mills— including seven of the nineteen erected after 1879—three of five sugar refineries, two of seven rope factories, one of three glass works, both of the Canadian steel mills, and six of the nation's twelve rolling mills."[37]

But all regions did not benefit or benefit equally from federal policy. Disaffection remained a latent regional political force which skilful provincial politicians, during periods of economic distress, could conjure up to frighten federal politicians into more benevolent behaviour. In 1886, for example, Nova

Scotia's premier, W. S. Fielding, fought and won a provincial election on the promise to substitute the federal tie for a Maritime regional government. Fielding, however, soon made his peace with industrialism and Central Canadian capital and became one of the staunchest proponents of the National Policy. In 1919, the federal government's reorganization of the Intercolonial Railway and its abolition of a favourable regional freight-rate structure triggered a similar movement to secure Maritime rights.[38] After a royal commission and a promise of more federal funds the movement lost its momentum.

Given Maritime union's separatist antecedents, it is perhaps somewhat ironic that the present movement was reborn at a convivial federal-provincial conference and backed by one of the region's staunchest federalist advocates. The contemporary movement's non-partisan support suggests its new respectability. The federal government has even proffered its blessing. In February 1965, a resolution of the Nova Scotia and New Brunswick legislatures called for the creation of a commission to study the feasibility of Maritime union. Under the chairmanship of J. J. Deutsch, the commission examined the effects of union on fiscal relations, medicare, education, the French language, and public opinion. To anyone familiar with the history of Maritime union the single sentence in the commission's preface to their printed report stating that "the involvement of the federal government was limited to financial aid and the provision of information . . ."[39] contains greater significance than the commissioners probably intended. It might well represent a reversal of the historic strategy of divide and rule. No longer a threat to Confederation, the cost benefits of Maritime union have perhaps begun to convince the most recalcitrant.

NOTES

1. Some of the more interesting are: J.M. Beck, *A History of Maritime Union* (Maritime Union Study, 1970); C.B. Fergusson, "Maritime Union," *Queen's Quarterly* (Summer 1970); J.F. Graham, "Should the Atlantic Provinces Unite?" in *Politics: Canada,* ed. P.W. Fox (Toronto, 1970).
2. Cape Breton was restored to Nova Scotia in 1820 and Prince Edward Island was rejoined briefly to Nova Scotia between the years 1784 and 1786.

3. Wilfred I. Smith, ed., "Charles Tupper's Minutes of the Charlottetown Conference," *Canadian Historical Review* (June 1967), pp. 101-12.

4. See the Hon. Joseph Howe, *'Confederation Considered in Relation to the Interests of the Empire'* (London, 1866).

5. The Catholic and Presbyterian churches were stalwart defenders of French and Gaelic and the Lutheran Church maintained German clergy as late as 1860.

6. D.C. Harvey, *An Introductory History of Dalhousie University* (Halifax, 1938), p. 9.

7. J.M. Beck, *Joseph Howe: Voice of Nova Scotia* (Toronto, 1964).

8. Margaret MacPhail, *Loch Bras D'Or* (Windsor, 1970), p. 161.

9. See G.A. Rawlyk, *Historical Essays on the Atlantic Provinces* (Toronto, 1967), p. 1.

10. J.B. Brebner, *New England's Outpost* (New York, 1927).

11. G.A. Rawlyk, *Nova Scotia's Massachusetts* (Montreal, 1973).

12. Jean Daigle, "Les commerçants-entrepreneur acadiens et le Massachusetts à la fin du 17e siècle" (unpublished paper presented to le Congrès annuel de l'Institut d'Histoire de l'Amérique française, 17 octobre 1975).

13. Thomas H. Raddall, *His Majesty's Yankees* (New York, 1942).

14. Canada, *Census of Canada, 1871,* Vol. IV, contains summaries of census material on the Maritime provinces from 1687 to 1869. All figures presented in this essay come from the 1861 printed census return.

15. G.A. Rawlyk and G. Stewart, "Nova Scotia's Sense of Mission," *Social History* (November 1968).

16. R. Baden Powell, "The Bay of Fundy Ferry," *Nova Scotia Historical Quarterly* (September 1972), p. 253.

17. *McAlpine's Maritime Directory, 1870-71,* p. 693.

18. *The Rowell/Sirois Report, Book I,* ed. Donald V. Smiley (Toronto, 1963), p. 18.

19. Alton A. Lomas, "The Industrial Development of Nova Scotia, 1830-1854" (MA thesis, Dalhousie University, 1950), p. 19.

20. G.S. Graham, "The Gypsum Trade in the Maritime Provinces: Its Relation to American Diplomacy in the Early Nineteenth Century," *Agricultural History* (July 1938).

21. Lomas, "Industrial Development," pp. 98, 104, and 132.

22. D.A. Muise, "Shipping and Ship-Building in the Maritimes Provinces in the 19th Century," *Visual History Series,* p. 3.

23. G.V. Shand, "Windsor, a Centre of Shipbuilding," *Collections of the Nova Scotia Historical Society,* Vol. 37 (1970), p. 50.

24. Lomas, "Industrial Development", p. 277.

25. T.C. Haliburton, *Sam Slick the Clockmaker* (Toronto, 1941), p. 46.

26. George MacLaren, "Communications in the Northumberland Strait and the Gulf of St. Lawrence, 1775-1925," *Nova Scotia Historical Quarterly* (June 1951), p. 102.

27. R.M. Guy, "The Industrial Development and Urbanization of Pictou County, Nova Scotia to 1900" (MA thesis, Acadia University, 1962), p. 29.

28. *The McAlpine Maritime Directory, 1870-71,* p. 1299.
29. George MacLaren, "The Pictou Literary and Scientific Society," *Nova Scotia Historical Quarterly* (June 1973), p. 100.
30. Lomas, "Industrial Development," p. 86.
31. R.M. Guy, "Urbanization of Pictou County," p. 18.
32. Ibid., p. 100.
33. A.G. Bailey, "Railway and the Confederation Issue in New Brunswick, 1863-1865," *Canadian Historical Review* (December 1940), p. 367.
34. See W.H. Whitelaw, *The Maritimes and Canada Before Confederation* (Toronto, 1966), pp. 161-62.
35. For a full discussion of the Confederation debate in Nova Scotia, see D.A. Muise, "The Federal Election of 1867 in Nova Scotia: An Economic Interpretation," *Collections of the Nova Scotia Historical Society,* Vol. 36 (1968); and "Parties and Constituencies: Federal Elections in Nova Scotia, 1867-1896," *Historical Papers,* 1971.
36. P.B. Waite, *Arduous Destiny* (Toronto, 1971), p. 56.
37. T.W. Acheson, "The National Policy and the Industrialization of the Maritimes: 1880-1910," *Acadiensis* (Spring 1972), p. 14.
38. E.R.T. Forbes, "The Origins of the Maritime Rights Movement," *Acadiensis* (Autumn 1975).
39. *Maritime Union Study* (Fredericton, 1970), pp. 6-7.

ERNEST R. FORBES

Misguided Symmetry: The Destruction of Regional Transportation Policy for the Maritimes*

In analysing and recounting the development of Canadian transportation policy, economists have invariably had trouble explaining the source and nature of the Maritime provinces' chronic transportation grievances. Their problem has been compounded by a dearth of historical research on the modern period of Maritime history and the fact that the Board of Railway Commissioners, whose judgments provide their traditional source of information, did not have official jurisdiction over the Intercolonial Railway until 1923. Most major studies, including those by A. W. Currie and H. L. Purdy, begin with the report of the Duncan Commission of 1926 or the Maritime Freight Rates Act of 1927.[1] These documents, however, represent the end rather than the beginning of the most decisive period for the Maritimes in the development of national transportation policy.

* The focus of this essay is upon the original two Maritime provinces, Nova Scotia and New Brunswick. By the 1920s, however, Prince Edward Island, despite a preoccupation with its own unique transportation grievances, had made common cause with the two larger provinces in a campaign for regional transportation "rights." Newfoundland, although superficially associated with the Maritimes through its inclusion in the Maritime Freight Rates Act subsidies in 1949, is a separate region both in terms of historical experience and contemporary transportation needs, and is not considered in this study.

In the preceding decade the federal government had destroyed a regionally oriented rate structure which had made possible much of the region's industrial development over the previous forty years and replaced it with one unsuited to Maritime needs and foreign to the Maritime experience.

The Maritimes' traditional transportation policy was a product of the Intercolonial Railway and the unique circumstances of its construction. Built and operated as a public project far in advance of any reasonable hope for success as a commercial enterprise, the railway lacked sufficient traffic to meet operating expenses, much less provide a return on capital invested. As the sine qua non of their entry into Confederation, Maritime statesmen regarded it as an instrument of national and regional development, its primary function being the provision of competitive access for Maritime products in Central Canadian markets.[2] Both the railway's traffic needs and the Maritimers' commercial aspirations converged in the creation of a low and flexible rate structure designed to foster the development of Maritime industry. Even after the entry of other railways into the Maritimes, the Intercolonial remained the rate-maker for the region; other lines had to match its low developmental rates to remain competitive.

The opening of the West through a privately owned commercial road led to the development there of a very different transportation policy. The government confined its involvement in the construction of the Canadian Pacific Railway largely to the bestowal of gifts: land grants, tax concessions, and a guaranteed monopoly in its western territory. The last, not surprisingly, encouraged Westerners to believe that they were the victims of unjustifiably high rates—a conviction which lingered after the formal monopoly ended. Partly to escape the brunt of western anger, the government created a semi-judicial Board of Railway Commissioners to regulate rates on private lines.

As the Grand Trunk Pacific and Canadian Northern Railway systems neared bankruptcy early in the twentieth century and as the West grew in political influence and militancy, governments, railway management, and commissioners became increasingly defensive in their formulation of transportation policy. They tended to give two principles precedence over all others in rate-making: rates must be high enough to provide a "reasonable" return on capital prudently invested; and "discrimination" through the maintenance of different levels in different parts of the country must be eliminated. Their purpose was, obviously, to protect the railway's profits on one hand and to assuage the Westerners' sense of grievance on the other. In the achievement of these goals, they were prepared to sacrifice virtually all other considerations in rate-making, including industrial development, the conquest of geographical barriers, and the cultivation of traffic. The result was a transportation policy which had as its central feature the creation of a rigid, artificial, and sterile rate symmetry.

The sudden extension to the Maritimes of this policy—the very antithesis of the principles upon which the Intercolonial had developed—was a major factor in the disruption of the Maritimes' economy in the early 1920s. It remained an obstacle to the region's recovery in succeeding decades. Understandably, Maritimers tended to focus their efforts at rehabilitating their economy on those factors in its decline over which their governments had some control. For half a century they attempted, with limited success, to modify or escape the rigidity of the alien rate structure in order to restore "their" railway as an instrument of regional development. Only recently, with the apparent disintegration of the structure from other causes, does it again appear possible to return to a transportation policy based, at least in part, upon a rational consideration of regional needs.

Initially burdened with a circuitous route dictated by political and strategic circumstances, and chronically short of traffic, the Intercolonial quickly justified the predictions of its detractors that it would not "pay for the grease on the axles of its carriages."[3] In the first fifteen years of operation it amassed a net operating deficit of over four million dollars. In addition, its capital account grew steadily and was recorded in departmental reports side by side with comparable federal investment in the canal systems of Ontario and Quebec.

In attempting to cope with the Intercolonial's deficits, successive governments followed a policy of expansion through the development of spur lines within the Maritimes and the extension of the railway westward from its original terminus at Rivière du Loup.[4] Simultaneously they developed a rate structure much lower than that in force on Central Canadian lines, especially on long-haul traffic. In both expansion and rate-making, the interests of transportation and national policy neatly coalesced. At a time when the traditional Maritime economy, based upon wood, wind, and sail, was in eclipse, and many of the outports of the region were in sharp decline, the railway offered manufacturing industries access to new markets in Central and later in Western Canada.

The full impact of the lower rate structure was not felt until the Intercolonial reached Montreal in 1898. At this point the Intercolonial became the undisputed rate-maker between the Maritimes and Central Canada. It determined the transportation costs which Maritime producers had to absorb in competing with their Central Canadian rivals, both in the latter's own markets and in Western Canada. The basic or standard mileage rates appeared to be designed to extend the competitive range of Maritime products and thus encourage the development of long-haul traffic on the road. Rates for up to 100 miles were approximately 20 per cent lower than on Central Canadian lines; but for over 400 miles they were more than 30 per cent lower, and for 700 miles more than 50 per cent lower.[5] On traffic destined for markets west of Montreal the Maritime manufacturer enjoyed fixed arbitrary rates on the Maritime to Montreal portion which gave him a stable relationship with his Central Canadian competitors. If these rates failed to move goods, even lower rates might be negotiated on an ad hoc basis at the Moncton headquarters. Such rates were not restricted to large producers; even station agents were given discretion in fixing rates for distances of less than 100 miles. C.N.R. Vice-President J. E. Dalrymple subsequently attested to the flexibility of the system in the sarcastic comment that "practically every Tom, Dick and Harry down in the Maritimes could make any rate he wanted to make."[6]

Built into the rate structure in the Maritimes was a differential in eastbound over westbound rates. In other words, the Maritime shipper could export his products to Central Canada or further west at about 12 per cent less than it cost the Central Canadians to reciprocate.[7] This differential was not unique to the Intercolonial, but was a basic feature of the North American rate structure. Its function had been the diversion of exports through New York and Montreal, and the assistance of New England and Maritime manufacturers in competing in western markets.[8] In practice it enabled the railway to maintain low rates to encourage Maritime exports, without unduly sacrificing revenues from established traffic moving in the opposite direction, and it provided Maritime producers with an element of "protection" in their local markets.

The policy of flexibility and low rates was effective in reducing the Intercolonial's deficits. In the first five years after the railway was extended to Montreal, freight tonnage doubled; in the first fifteen years, it quadrupled. The pattern of almost continuous operating deficits was broken. In 1899, the Intercolonial recorded its first significant surplus and thereafter tended to offset deficits with compensating surpluses. Between 1897 and 1917, the railway showed a net operating surplus of $320,334.[9]

Not only did such freight-rate policies help the Intercolonial's finances but they permitted the industrialization of the Maritimes to a degree seldom recognized by Canadian historians. As T. W. Acheson has shown, in the 1880s Nova Scotia's per-capita growth in manufacturing was the highest in the country; Saint John's exceeded that of Hamilton.[10] Moreover, such policies enabled the Maritimes to share in the general economic expansion which accompanied the rapid development of Western Canada. Much of the Intercolonial's increased tonnage came from the growth of secondary manufacturing in the towns along the railway. Between 1900 and 1920, Nova Scotia's capital investment in manufacturing increased over 400 per cent to $148.3 million while New Brunswick's multiplied five times to $109.5 million.[11] The population in most of the leading towns along the road, including Moncton, Amherst, New Glasgow, and Sydney, virtually doubled within the same period.[12] The growth of the coal-steel industry was spectacular. Pig iron production multiplied seventeen times between 1900 and 1913.[13] Two large vertically-integrated corporations, Dominion Iron and Steel and Nova Scotia Steel and Coal, not only produced the basic metals but continued the manufacturing process in their rolling mills, foundries, and machine shops to turn out a variety of items ranging from barbed wire to railway cars.[14] Maritime products—stoves, furniture, pianos, mining cars, soaps, shoes, textiles, confectioneries, and even a few farm tractors—found their way to the Prairies and British Columbia. Aided by low freight rates, cheap sources of energy, the tariff, and a booming national economy, Maritime manufacturers secured a large hinterland in Central and Western Canada to absorb the volume necessary for competitive production.[15]

While the Maritimes enjoyed undoubted benefits from the Intercolonial's regionally oriented transportation policy, their ability to defend it declined steadily as their political influence waned. In the 1890s, the region held 18 per cent of the seats in the federal House of Commons; by 1914, its representation had dropped to 13 per cent. The balance of power shifted westward with the growth in Western representation from 8 to 24 per cent. In their fight to overcome their own transportation difficulties, Western leaders led an agitation to equalize freight rates. By 1916, the Board of Railway Commissioners accepted the principle of a "reasonable" rate parity between East and West, while maintaining the rule that rates should be high enough to provide a "reasonable" return on capital invested.[16] Caught between the West's demand for equalization and the need to justify increases to help private railway operators, the federal government found the lower rates on the Intercolonial an acute embarrassment.

In an era of progressive reform, the Intercolonial was vulnerable for its image of patronage, partisanship, and corruption. The reputation was not altogether deserved. The Intercolonial was probably no more or less patronage-ridden than many other publicly owned projects in the nineteenth century. It was caught in no major political scandals. But opposition members from the Maritimes regularly washed its dirty linen in the House in an attempt to score debating points for use in their region against the government. Even though the Intercolonial eliminated the grosser forms of patronage by the second decade of the twentieth century—political firings were abolished by formal agreement with the railway unions and manager David Pottinger strenuously resisted appointments or promotions which might tend to undermine the efficiency of the road—the public was slow to accept the reality of the change.[17] Criticism continued from such diverse motives as political partisanship, progressive sentiment, opposition to public ownership, and regional jealousy.

The attack on the Intercolonial's rate structure began soon after the Borden government's accession to office. In 1912, complaints from Central Canadian manufacturers led to the abolition of the East-West differential.[18] In 1917, R. B. Bennett, speaking as "a western man," scathingly denounced the burden of the Intercolonial's deficits upon the Canadian taxpayer. Claiming that its rates were "from 25 to 78 per cent less than those we pay upon the plains for the same services," he demanded that the Intercolonial's rates be brought under the jurisdiction of the railway commissioners.[19] Later in the session the government introduced an amendment to the Railway Act to do just that.

The bill encountered strong resistance from Maritime members. They protested bitterly that their people had not been given sufficient warning of a measure which would place the regulation of their freight rates under an external body lacking intimate knowledge of the needs of their railway or their industries. Not only would Maritime businesses lose the convenience of easy consultation with rate-making authorities, but the government might use the board as a "wicked partner" in dismantling the Intercolonial's rate structure.[20] The bill passed all three readings but, in the face of implacable opposition from the Maritimes, was not proclaimed.

The Maritimers' victory was short lived. In the spring of 1917, the Drayton-Acworth Commission, investigating the problems of the near-bankrupt Canadian Northern and Grand Trunk railways, recommended their integration with the government railways in a single publicly owned system. In an attempt to make the dose more palatable for Maritimers, the commissioners recognized the traditionally lower rate levels of the region and recommended, somewhat disingenously, that these not be altered without the approval of the railway commissioners.[21] In November 1918, an Order-in-Council placed the Intercolonial under the management of the board of directors responsible for the Canadian Northern Railway.

Under the direction of D. B. Hanna, former manager of the Canadian Northern, the Maritimers' worst fears were realized. The new management dismantled the Moncton headquarters, moving clerical staff to Toronto, transferred top Intercolonial officials to other lines, and demolished the intricate rate structure developed over the previous forty years.[22] They ignored the manufacturers' "arbitraries," applying the full weight of the large increases necessitated by wartime inflation to all portions of Maritime rates. They cancelled the special commodity rates on coal and sugar and began raising Maritime rates to a par with those in Ontario and Quebec. Such increases came just in time to provide an inflated base for the application of the 40 per cent increase of September 1920.[23]

These changes were not dictated by any careful study of the needs of Maritime railways. In part, they appeared as little discussed footnotes to the problem of the bankrupt lines. The inclusion of the Intercolonial was perhaps a logical step in the creation of a nationally integrated railway system, but the manner in which all regional variations were eliminated from the Maritime rates suggested the government's concern to alleviate Western jealousy. Publicly, the new management appeared to bask in the righteous glow of having eliminated a patronage-ridden political football. D. B. Hanna shrugged off all Maritime protests as attempts to restore patronage on the line. Such a response made an excellent smokescreen for combatting Maritime criticism.[24]

Maritime producers were, however, directing their attack at the economic effects of an alien rate structure. In the debate on the Railway Act of 1919, Maritime members of Parliament argued that, since the Intercolonial was built as part of the original Confederation agreement, it should not be included in a general system whose rates were determined by the need for a return on capital. Their amendment to that effect was defeated, although the railway minister promised to preserve a separate system of accounts for their line.[25] In the summer of 1919, Maritime businessmen led a delegation to Ottawa to protest the disruption in their rate schedules. When the government turned a deaf ear, they revived the moribund Maritime Board of Trade as the chief agency of their agitation.[26] By mid-decade, the board, with the financial support of the three provincial governments, established a freight rates committee (later commission) and retained an "expert" to aid in the preparation of their case.[27]

In their initial appeals before the Board of Railway Commissioners, Maritimers pointed out the disastrous effect of the rate increases on their industries and argued again the injustice of suddenly applying commercial rates to what had been essentially a non-commercial road. The Intercolonial was, in the words of Sir John A. Macdonald, "a political consequence of political union." Its purpose was the consolidation of Confederation and the development of interprovincial trade. "From 1874 to 1916," stated their spokesman, E. M. Macdonald, "every political party in power in this country, every Minister of Railways, everyone who had anything to do with the operation of the railway recognized that it was a railway that should be dealt with on that basis."[28] But the Maritimers made no progress against the board's reaffirmation of the doctrine of rate equalization. The commissioners had ruled specifically that rates could not be lowered to aid industrial development nor to overcome geographical disadvantages.[29] Moreover, claims regarding the original purpose of the road were beyond the scope of the commissioners' deliberations. "We have nothing to do with any of the political conditions, or with very much of the past history," stated the chief commissioner in 1920. "We are trying to consider this matter purely from legal and business standpoints." For other aspects of their case, Maritimers would have to "go to the government."[30]

Go to the government they did in the summer of 1920. The provincial legislatures of Nova Scotia and New Brunswick passed identical, unanimous resolutions affirming: "that the faithful observation of the terms and conditions of the compact of confederation and a generous national spirit require that the convenience, accommodation and welfare of the people and of the industrial interest of the Maritime Provinces be steadily kept in view as the primary purpose to be achieved in the administration of the Intercolonial Railway. And that such railway having been constructed to serve a special purpose should be administrated upon principles adapted to effect such purpose and as a separate system, giving such advantages in freight and other rates to the people of the Maritime Provinces as will afford them access to the markets of the Dominion upon such terms as will admit them to fair competition."[31] A conference of boards of trade, shipping, manufacturing, cooperative, and farming groups passed a similar resolution and sponsored a fifty-man delegation to present their case to the federal cabinet.[32]

Some of the strongest support for the Maritimes' case came, strangely enough, from A. E. Kemp, a prominent Toronto manufacturer and Minister without Portfolio in the Meighen government. In a confidential memorandum for his colleagues in the cabinet, Kemp compared the traditional rate-making policies in the Maritimes to those of the regional railways in the United States which had tailored their rates to the needs of local industry. Despite its talk of rate-equalization, the Interstate Commerce Commission had respected such regional variations in its decisions. But in Canada the railways "in their anxiety ... to secure more revenue" had "entirely overlooked" the fact that only by their encouragement were Maritime manufacturers "able to obtain markets for their products which are now found in all the Western Provinces of the Dominion." In allowing the increases, the railway commissioners had failed "to differentiate where territorial necessity demanded." Since they had regarded questions of "broad national policy" beyond the scope of their deliberations, it was clearly the responsibility of the federal government to intervene. While it was, perhaps, too late for "radical" changes, the government should, Kemp argued, protect Maritime industries from the more drastic effects of the commissioners' error by exempting the region from the projected 40 per cent increase. [33]

Kemp's cogent advice went unheeded by his colleagues in the Meighen cabinet. "It would be rank sectionalism," commented a press release from Conservative party headquarters, "to lower rates in one part of the country and keep them up in another."[34] The ideal of symmetry in the national rate structure would be preserved no matter what the cost to Maritime industry.

That cost proved to be substantial. Between 1917 and the end of 1920, cumulative rate increases in Central Canada, largely necessitated by wartime inflation, totalled 111 per cent; in the Maritimes, these increases, combined with the levelling up of the Intercolonial's rates, led to raises of from 140 to 216 per cent.[35] The increases adversely affected virtually all aspects of the Maritime economy. Farmers complained that freight costs often exceeded the price of vegetables in markets where they had been traditionally sold. Fish merchants blamed rates for depressing the fresh fish industry. Sugar refineries cut back heavily in production and laid off workers. Manufacturers who were still able to retain a share of the national market, such as Moirs chocolates, Simms brushes, and Enterprise stoves, found their handicap in transportation costs relative to their Montreal and/or Toronto competitors just about doubled.[36]

The increases came at a critical time for heavy manufacturing in the Maritimes. Here, as elsewhere, industry had been diverted to munition production during the war. At the war's end new investment was required to retool plants for peace-time needs. But the sudden deterioration of the Maritime position in transportation made such investment less attractive. The two large steel corporations, which in 1920 had united in the British Empire Steel Corporation, failed to modernize and were very close to bankruptcy by mid-decade.[37] In 1921, the Canadian Car and Foundry Company of Amherst and the Maritime Nail Company of Saint John began to transfer their operations to Montreal.[38] One company which initially defied the trend, Robb Engineering of Amherst, reorganized its plant for the large-scale production of farm tractors for sale in the Prairies. It entered into an agreement with the Montreal Bridge Company whereby it would supply the engines and more sophisticated parts while Montreal Bridge provided wheels, frames, and final assembly at its Winnipeg branch. Confronted with the 40 per cent rate increase and the complete removal of the 20 per cent tariff on farm tractors costing less than $1,400, [39] they halted production at about a hundred vehicles. By mid-decade, Robb

Engineering was reduced to servicing earlier lines of products still in use. J. A. Robb reported in 1926 that he had laid off 350 of his 400 highly trained employees, the majority of whom had found jobs in the United States.[40]

Such job losses were general in the Maritimes in the early 1920s. From 1919 to 1921 the total employed in manufacturing in the region declined by nearly twenty thousand or about 42 per cent.[41] For many, the decline was permanent. In 1926, eight of the leading industrial towns and cities along the Intercolonial provided 45 per cent fewer jobs in manufacturing than they had at the beginning of the decade.[42] At the same time, approximately 150,000 Maritimers left the region.[43]

This is not to suggest, of course, that freight rates alone were responsible for the Maritimes' problems. The postwar recession was an international phenomenon. With the greater development of hydroelectric power and changes in the coal tariff, the Maritimes lost their advantage in energy costs. But the rate changes were a major factor in both the original collapse of the Maritime economy and its failure to recover after 1923. Not only did they help undermine the competitive position of existing Maritime industry, but they permanently discouraged the location within the region of new industry dependent upon markets elsewhere in the country.

Ironically, the drastic rate increases did not improve the financial position of the railways, and in the long term probably injured it. Although the initial cumulative "horizontal" increases of 42 per cent in 1918 were efficient in a buoyant economy and yielded proportionate increases in revenue, the continued levelling up of local rates and an additional 40 per cent increase in 1920 were followed by a decline in traffic on the line of about 40 per cent (compared with 19 per cent nationally) and a drop in total revenue of 17 per cent.[44] The slump in traffic lingered. Despite drastic layoffs, curtailment in services, and centralization of management at Toronto, the annual deficits, which had begun just prior to the increases of 1918, rose steadily. For the year ending March 1920 they were $2.3 million, for 1921, $3.1 million, and for 1922, $3.7 million.[45] Although hidden from the public after the reorganization in 1923, the operating deficits for the Atlantic region were five million for that year, three and one-half million in 1924, and three million in 1925.[46] In the first seven years of centralized control, the net operating deficits on the Atlantic lines were more than triple those of the Intercolonial in its forty-one years of independent operation. While inflation, reorganization, and changing economic circumstances invalidate a direct comparison, the fact remains that centralization, although adding to the burden of Maritime industry, did not ease the burden for the Canadian taxpayer.

Maritimers' anger at the loss of a positive regional transportation policy at so critical a time for their industries found political expression as the central issue of the Maritime Rights Movement, a regional protest agitation which swept all three provinces in the 1920s. On visiting the Maritimes before the election of 1921, Arthur Meighen found party organization a shambles and regional sentiment mobilizing in an anti-government protest. Hastily, he "consulted" leading railway officials by telegraph and then, over their opposition, announced a new policy of "decentralization" in C.N.R. management.[47] With no sign of the policy being implemented before the election, his statement was not taken seriously by Maritime voters. Liberal candidates, claiming to have the support of W. L. Mackenzie King in their fight for Maritime transportation "rights," swept twenty-five of the region's thirty-one seats.[48]

In Ottawa, Maritime representatives found their goal of restoring traditional transportation policy an elusive one. King recorded in his diary how they came before him in an "ugly and belligerent spirit." Denying that he had made any specific promises on the issue, King claimed he could not act in the matter without risking defeat in the House.[49] From the Liberal Toronto *Star,* Maritime members received a lecture on the dangers of "sectionalism" and attempts at "political blackmail."[50] Nevertheless, the government did follow through with a partial regionalization of the C.N.R. along the lines suggested by Arthur Meighen. Each of four divisions received separate bookkeeping entries and a local management with its headquarters within the region. What they did not obtain, however, was authority to develop a regional policy in rate-making. Here centralization was as rigid as ever, as all proposed rate changes had to be forwarded to Montreal for approval lest rates in any one region provide a basis for forcing them down in others. According to A. T. Weldon, general manager of the Atlantic Division, the regional management had learned "from sad experience" they were not permitted to adjust rates below the levels in force in the rest of the country.[51]

Maritime anger was in no way blunted by the new division. The truncation of the Intercolonial at Lévis, Quebec, revealed that the region was farther than ever from securing separate control of the critical Maritimes to Montreal portion of its export rates. Again Maritime voters demonstrated their resentment of government transportation and other regional policies in a spectacular swing to the opposition. Proclaiming themselves champions of Maritime rights, Conservative candidates won twenty-three of the regions' twenty-eight seats in the federal election of 1925.[52]

Continued political pressure from the Maritimes and a growing sentiment in the rest of the country that "something" would have to be done about the economic problems of the region led to a reasonably objective analysis of the role of transportation in Maritime difficulties. Early in 1926, Mackenzie King appointed a royal commission to investigate Maritime claims. Headed and dominated by Sir Andrew Rae Duncan, a British lawyer with considerable executive and supervisory experience in industrial affairs, the commissioners heard extensive testimony from Maritime businessmen, their freight-rates expert, F. C. Cornell, and various railway officials including C.N.R. President Sir Henry Thornton. They also held private interviews with the railway commissioners and commissioned confidential memoranda. Their conclusions upheld the essence of the Maritime argument. It was not fair, they agreed, to have encouraged industries to locate in the Maritimes dependent upon one type of transportation policy—one closely related to national policy—and then allow them to be destroyed by the adoption of an entirely different policy. It was not fair to the industries and certainly not in the national interest.[53]

The commissioners' remedy was intended to meet the requirements of the region and to overcome the main objections of the railways. The rates on the Maritime lines, the commissioners recommended, should be restored to approximately the level relative to rates in the rest of the country which had existed prior to 1912. This, they suggested, could be accomplished by reducing rates by 20 per cent both on traffic within the region, and on the Maritimes-to-Lévis portion of westbound rates on exports from the region. By exempting rates on eastbound traffic originating from outside the region from the reduction, they could restore the differential eliminated in 1912. The railway officials had warned that concessions to the Maritimes might "raise a clamour which would be difficult to arrest for similar assistance elsewhere" and "might well seriously affect and perhaps disrupt not only the freight structure of Canada but the freight rate structure of the North American continent."[54] To meet this objection, the commissioners called for separate legislation which would prohibit the use of the lower Maritime rates by other regions as a basis for claims of discrimination. They also adopted Sir Henry Thornton's suggestion that the cost of the reductions should be borne by the national government through a direct subsidy to the railway.

The commissioners did not stop with a call for specific reductions but attempted to restore the element of flexibility so necessary for the development of a regional transportation policy. They were highly critical of a system which failed to allow consideration by the rate-making authority of the effect of the rates on the industrial development of the country. Agreeing with the need to preserve an adequate return for the railways, they proposed that the Board of Railway Commissioners be empowered to order investigations, authorize experimental rates, and fix rates at levels which would both provide adequate compensation to the road and encourage interprovincial trade. The rates set for this purpose, they argued, should not be considered grounds for claims of discrimination from other parts of the road.

Although Mackenzie King had promised to implement the Duncan Commission's findings,[55] his cabinet was unhappy with a program which tampered with the basic rate structure. Early in 1927, the Toronto *Globe* told of dissension within the cabinet and predicted the implementation of the railway clauses of the commission's recommendations would be postponed.[56] This report touched off a revival of agitation by Maritime boards of

trade. After a flying trip to Ottawa, the Maritime Board of
Trade Secretary, F. Maclure Sclanders, reported that the railways constituted a major source of opposition to Duncan's proposals.[57] Late in March, the cabinet reached a compromise
which included the implementation of the reductions for the
Maritimes, but left out all reference to the proposed extension
in the responsibilities of the Board of Railway Commissioners.[58]
In 1927, the Maritime Freight Rates Act (M.F.R.A.) proclaimed
the regional producers' right of access to "the larger market of
the whole Canadian people" and restored a basically lower
freight-rate structure within and from the three Maritime provinces. It did not, however, restore the flexibility which had
permitted a selective adjustment of rates to stimulate trade and
industrial development. Nor did it protect Maritime producers
from a centralizing bias in the system which would later destroy
the advantage provided by the Act.

Within a few years, the Maritime producers discovered a new
and insidious threat to their position in the national rate structure. One exception in the goal of rate symmetry which the railway commissioners regularly tolerated was the need of meeting
competition from other kinds of transportation. For example,
lower rates were traditionally justified in Central and Eastern
Canada as necessary to meet water competition on the St.
Lawrence system. The birth of the trucking industry added a
new dimension of competition to which, because of their class
rate structure based upon value as well as weight,[59] the railways
were particularly vulnerable. While they enjoyed the status of a
monopoly, they had been able to force internal subsidization
between high and low priced commodities. But truckers, independent of rate regulation, could "cream" the low-weight, high-
value traffic, leaving to the railways only the bulkier, less
profitable share of the trade. In meeting this competition, railway rates were frequently lowered or held down. In 1938, the
government authorized a new type of competitive rate, the
agreed charge, by which a railway contracted to move all or a
portion of a firm's products at a fixed rate over a given period.
Since trucking had its earliest and most successful development

in the densely settled parts of Central Canada, rates were reduced there while being raised to recoup revenue in the peripheral regions.

Maritimers desperately sought to make the new competitive rates the basis for their reductions under the M.F.R.A., but without success. In 1933, both the Board of Railway Commissioners and the Supreme Court of Canada rejected their claim.[60] After the Second World War, the repeated rate increases, usually limited in Central Canada by the need to meet competition, undermined the competitive position of their industry. The Maritimers' appeal to a federal royal commission, the Turgeon Commission of 1951, met rejection in a terse statement that the M.F.R.A. was a "once and for all" measure which "has performed all the functions for which it was designed."[61]

The deterioration in the relative position of Maritime shippers accelerated rapidly in the 1950s. Between 1948 and the end of 1958, increases on authorized rates totaled 157 per cent.[62] While the increases were the same on these rates in all parts of the country, the actual burden of the increases was considerably less in Central Canada where a higher proportion of the traffic moved at competitive rates. An analysis of 1 per cent of the railway waybills for 1958 revealed that 52 per cent of Central Canada's rail traffic moved at competitive or agreed charge rates, compared with only 35 per cent for the Maritimes. By 1964, the total had grown to 43 per cent for the Maritimes, but had jumped to 70 per cent for Central Canada.[63]

A few examples indicate the effect of this trend upon the competitive position of Maritime industry. In 1951, steel bars from Amherst had reached Quebec City at an advantage in transportation costs of 4 per cent a ton over those of a Montreal competitor. In 1954, a new competitive rate from Montreal dropped the advantage to minus-75 per cent. By 1964, it was down to minus-100 per cent. In 1953, electric stoves travelling from Sackville to Montreal had an advantage of 56 per cent over a Hamilton competitor. With the advent of a new competitive rate in 1955, the advantage suddenly became a disadvantage of 30 per cent.[64] A similar deterioration in the Maritime shippers' position was apparent in the cases of such products as canned fruit, meats, vegetables, and steel billots.[65]

Not until 1957 did the federal government recognize the new

crisis for Maritime industry. Prodded by the Gordon Commission on Canada's economic prospects, it increased the subsidy on interregional traffic from the Maritimes from 20 to 30 per cent.[66] By then, Maritimers had begun to realize that continued attempts to alleviate their shippers' problems by increasing the subsidy would be self-defeating. The subsidies had become a cumbersome and inefficient tool for aiding the Maritime producer. Since the reductions were made from the authorized rates, which moved only a portion of Canadian traffic, much of the subsidy was in fact going into railway coffers without affording comparable benefits to Maritime producers. Indeed, by yielding lower rates at no cost to the railway, the subsidies tended to discourage the development of trucking competition within the Maritimes.

Another federal royal commission, the MacPherson Commission of 1961, suggested a revision of the M.F.R.A. subsidy program as part of a basic revision of Canadian transportation policy. The commissioners proposed to solve the railways' problem of competition by allowing them to adjust their rates more freely in pursuit of traffic and profits. With an optimism worthy of eighteenth-century Physiocrats, they found a panacea for Canada's transportation problems in the interplay of competition among different transportation modes. Alterations in transportation policy for purposes of national policy should, they argued, be recognized as such, paid for from the federal treasury, and applied equally to all carriers. In keeping with these principles, the commissioners suggested that the M.F.R.A. subsidies be applied to trucking as well as rail traffic from the region, with the necessary additional revenue to be derived from the elimination of subsidies on movements within the region.[67] A British consulting firm subsequently endorsed their proposal in a more specific study of the Atlantic provinces' transportation facilities commissioned by the federal government.[68]

In passing the National Transportation Act in 1967, which was based upon the principles of the MacPherson report, the government took the novel step of inviting the Atlantic provinces to prepare their own recommendations for new legislation to replace the M.F.R.A., The outstanding feature of the four premiers' joint proposal of March 1969 was the call for "a federal-provincial agency" to "administer transportation assistance from federal funds to selected industries within the Atlantic Provinces."[69] That summer the government passed a new act, the Atlantic Region Freight Assistance Act, to permit the revision of the M.F.R.A., and the following year appointed the Federal-Provincial Committee on Atlantic Region Transportation to recommend how such funds as were available might be used most effectively to the advantage of the region. The personnel of the committee, which was suggestive of the committee's purpose in combining transportation and development goals, consisted of representatives from the Department of Transport, the Department of Regional Economic Expansion, each of the four Atlantic provinces, and Quebec. Within two years it had devised a program to apply subsidies to both truck and rail movements, to phase out the internal subsidies, and to channel the money saved into additional, selectively applied subsidies for industries attempting to penetrate national markets. By the end of 1974 it had reduced internal subsidies from 20 to 15 per cent and had prepared a list of commodities, suitable for promoting regional economic growth, which would receive special additional subsidies of 20 per cent on the traditional portion of westbound rates from the region.[70]

By creating the regional committee and implementing its recommendations, the government recognized three principles implicit in the operation of the old Intercolonial: the importance of regional input in transportation policy; the need for selectivity in rate-making; and the necessity of relating transportation policy to the requirements of regional economic development. But enlightened as the government's new policy has been in bringing much-needed reform to the old M.F.R.A. subsidies, it still side-steps the basic problem of the effect upon the Maritimes of a rate structure freed to fluctuate according to the dictates of competition. For with their isolation and smaller population the Maritimes can never expect to generate an intensity in transportation competition comparable to that of the larger centres in Central Canada. Indeed, one can only predict that the greater freedom granted railways through the National Transportation Act will accelerate the growth of Central

Canada's advantage in transportation and further undermine existing industry within the Maritimes.

This fact was forcefully brought home to Maritimers before the end of 1974. Preoccupied with improving the efficiency of their transportation services through a reform of the old subsidy, the development of common trucking legislation within the region, and the establishment of a new transportation advisory service for their producers,[71] they again found themselves confronted with an assault on their basic position in the rate structure with the railways' announcement of general increases and the abolition of less-than-carload-lot rates. The latter was a particular blow to the small, specialized manufacturers common to the region as it forced them to turn to "express" rates for small shipments at several times the previous cost.[72] When they resorted to their traditional defence of an appeal to the Board of Transport Commissioners and delay through the courts, they found their way blocked by the new limitations on regulation imposed by the National Transportation Act.

Their appeals to the cabinet were little more satisfactory. Transport Minister Jean Marchand agreed with their premise that transportation should be used as an instrument for regional development, and he eventually offered to aid industries which could demonstrate serious damage from the termination of the less-than-carload-lot rates.[73] But missing from the minister's statement, at least as reported in the press, was an indication of how and by what agency considerations of national or regional development could be injected into transportation policy on a regular basis. How, in the interest of regional development, can Maritime industry be protected against a continuing deterioration of its position in transportation relative to their Central Canadian competitors? Clearly the railways, locked, since the suppression of the Intercolonial, in an adversarial relationship with the region, are not suitable agencies for this purpose.[74] Nor, with its regulatory powers trimmed by the National Transportation Act, is the Board of Transport Commissioners. The logical agency, combining the necessary developmental and transportation interests as well as a substantial regional input, would appear to be the Federal-Provincial Committee.

The designation of an effective agency, however, would not

in itself be sufficient to ensure the maintenance of a stable position for the Maritimes' industry in the national system of transportation. Also required is the enunciation of a basic goal or principle for the agency to follow in developing a regional transportation policy. If the government is serious in its intent of encouraging industries to locate in the Maritimes, it should guarantee them average transportation costs either the same as or at least bearing a fixed relationship to the average of those of their more centrally located competitors.

A recommendation of this nature was contained in the Maritime Provinces' Transportation Commission presentation to the MacPherson Commission in 1960.[75] It was easy then to ignore because comparisons of actual rates and traffic movements in different regions were difficult. The 1 per cent waybill sample employed by the Transportation Commission gave too narrow a basis for accuracy. But now, with the computer providing more complete and detailed waybill analysis, lack of data should not be the critical problem.[76] Moreover, it should be feasible for the regional committee to obtain, from the same source, sufficient information on movements within the Maritimes to assess with precision the impact of rate changes on different industries. This would enable it regularly to redress the balance in the interest of national policy. The Federal-Provincial Committee would thus take on the attributes of a benevolent regional czar. It would control and stabilize the transportation costs of Maritime industry in relation to those of competitors elsewhere in the country. It would adjust rates on a selective basis to give maximum aid to regional industry from the funds made available to pay the cost of national parity in Canadian transportation policy. In short, it would play a role similar to that of the Intercolonial management in a more successful era of Maritime development.

The Maritimers' grievance is easily understood. Their transportation aspirations have been consistent for over a century. They expected that the railway, promised them for their participation in Confederation, would be operated to their advantage as an instrument of regional and national development. And so it was for the first forty years. But with integration into the

C.N.R., the railway's developmental role was abruptly terminated, thus contributing to the disruption of the region's economy in the 1920s. Maritimers responded with an intensive protest in the Maritime Rights movement. Although temporarily defused by the illusory promise of the Duncan Commission and the M.F.R.A., the agitation on the question of transportation has continued, its goals articulated by the Maritime Freight Rates Commission and supported by sporadic outbursts of popular resentment. In submissions to railway commissioners, royal commissions, and other federal agencies, the basic Maritime demand has remained constant. For, despite all the talk of decentralization, special subsidies, and federal policies for regional development, the restoration of the railway as an agent for national and regional development has not been conceded. Meanwhile, the Maritimers' position with respect to transportation costs continues to deteriorate. Only recently, with the creation of the federal-provincial committee, have hopes arisen that transportation may again become a genuine instrument of regional or national development. Whether such hopes are well-founded or whether they were raised as a diversionary gambit to deflate Maritime opposition to a potentially damaging National Transportation Act remains to be seen. Maritime governments are now actively negotiating in an attempt to transform verbal statements by federal ministers into concrete policies along the lines of their traditional aspirations. Given their previous experience, however, Maritimers can be forgiven if they do not immediately shed a scepticism so often justified in the case of past "concessions" in transportation policy.

NOTES

1. A.W. Currie, *Economics of Canadian Transportation* (Toronto, 1954), pp. 87-88, 93-96; and *Canadian Transportation Economics* (Toronto, 1967), pp. 111-15; H.L. Purdy, *Transport Competition and Public Policy in Canada* (Vancouver, 1972), pp. 164-65. A more recent study, H.J. Darling, *The Structure of Railway Subsidies in Canada* (Toronto, 1974), although addressing itself directly to the problem, has been little more successful. A polemical attack on the use of transportation in promoting regional development, it interprets the Maritime agitation as an imitative reaction to the prairies' successful efforts in restoring the Crow's Nest Pass rates.

2. For an early example of such attitudes see D.A. Muise, "Elections and Constituencies: Federal Politics in Nova Scotia, 1867-1878" (PH.D. thesis, University of Western Ontario, 1971), p. 164. See also G.P. de T. Glazebrook, *A History of Transportation in Canada,* Vol. 11 (Toronto, 1964) pp. 19-25.

3. Quoted in "Delegation from the Maritime Provinces: Report of the Meeting with the Prime Minister and Members of the Government, June 1, 1921," R.B. Bennett Papers, Public Archives of Canada (hereafter, P.A.C.). See also Sandford Fleming, *The Intercolonial: A Historical Sketch* (Montreal, 1876), p. 275.

4. "Annual Report of the Department of Railways and Canals," 1897-98, *Sessional Papers,* 1899, No. 10, Part I, p. 4, and Part II, pp. 28, 43, and 44. Total mileage grew from 714 in 1876 to 1,315 in 1898 and to 1,526 by 1916. "Annual Report," 1915-16, ibid., 1917, No. 20, p. 401.

5. R.A.C. Henry et al., *Railway Freight Rates in Canada: A Study Prepared for the Royal Commission on Dominion-Provincial Relations* (Ottawa, 1939), pp. 266-68.

6. Evidence, Royal Commission on Maritime Claims, 1926, p. 2130, typescript, Atlantic Provinces Transportation Commission, Moncton.

7. Calculated from *Province of Nova Scotia: A Submission of Its Claim with Respect to Maritime Disabilities within Confederation as Presented to the Royal Commission* (Halifax, 1926), p. 119.

8. Evidence, Board of Railway Commissioners, 1926, pp. 6676-81 and 6685, typescript, P.A.C. (hereafter cited as Evidence, B.R.C.).

9. Calculated from "Annual Report," 1915-16, *Sessional Papers,* 1917, No. 20, p. 401, and 1916-17, ibid., 1918, No. 20, p. 21.

10. T.W. Acheson, "The National Policy and the Industrialization of the Maritimes, 1880-1910," *Acadiensis* (Spring 1972), pp. 3-4.

11. *Canada Year Book,* 1922-23, pp. 415-16.

12. *Sixth Census of Canada, 1921,* Vol. 1, Table 10.

13. S.A. Saunders, *The Economic History of the Maritime Provinces: A Study Prepared for the Royal Commission on Dominion-Provincial Relations* (Ottawa, 1939), p. 115.

14. W.J.A. Donald, *The Canadian Iron and Steel Industry* (New York, 1915), pp. 195-98.

15. Saunders, *Economic History,* pp. 27-29.
16. Currie, *Economics of Canadian Transportation,* p. 60.
17. See David Pottinger to Frank Cochrane, 4 November 1912, and Pottinger to A.W. Campbell, 29 January 1913, Intercolonial Letterbooks, Canadian National Railways Papers, P.A.C., "Being an Address by Mr. Geo. Yates . . . ," Arthur Meighen Papers, pp. 157485-89, P.A.C.; G.R. Stevens, *The Canadian National Railways,* Vol. II (Toronto, 1962), p. 275. For the more traditional version of Intercolonial patronage and "corruption" see A.R. Clarke, "The Intercolonial, Its Influence on Canadian Development" (MA thesis, Acadia University, 1953).
18. Evidence, B.R.C., 1926, p. 6697. It is ironic, of course, that changes in transportation policy most detrimental to the Maritimes should have taken place during the prime ministership of Robert Borden, a Nova Scotian by origin. In meeting the political exigencies of the day, especially in the area of interregional conflict, local patriotism was not apparent in the activities of this progressive premier.
19. *House of Commons Debates,* 1917, p. 787 (hereafter cited as *Debates*).
20. Ibid., 1917, p. 4354.
21. *Report of the Royal Commission to Inquire into Railways and Transportation* (Ottawa, 1917), pp. lxvi-ix.
22. *Busy East of Canada* (Sackville), June and July 1923.
23. Evidence B.R.C., 1926, p. 6732. For a report on the case of sugar, see Robert Borden Papers, pp. 131, 068-72, P.A.C.
24. Before the Railway Committee, Hanna claimed that "the criticism of the Canadian National Railways begins and ends east of Montreal." Halifax *Herald,* 27 May 1921. For an example of his explanation of this criticism and the innuendo with which he met it, see D.B. Hanna, *Trains of Recollection* (Toronto, 1924), pp. 256-62.
25. *Debates,* 1919, p. 2135.
26. *Busy East of Canada* (Sackville), September 1919.
27. F.M. Sclanders to D.R. Turnbull, 3 September 1925. Maritime Provinces' Freight Rate Commission Papers, Atlantic Provinces Freight Rate Commission, Moncton.
28. Evidence, B.R.C., 1920, p. 5336.
29. *Orders and Ruling of the Board of Railway Commissioners,* Vol. 13, p. 260, and *Canadian Railway Cases,* Vol. 14, p. 178.
30. Evidence, B.R.C., 1920, p. 11701.
31. New Brunswick, *Journals of the Legislative Assembly,* 1921, pp. 146-49; Nova Scotia, *Journal and Proceedings of the House of Assembly,* 1921, pp. 356-61.
32 *Busy East of Canada* (Sackville), May 1921.
33. Enclosure, A.E. Kemp to Meighen, 17 September 1920, Arthur Meighen Papers, P.A.C. See also Gerald Kraft, R. Meyer, and J.P. Valette, *The Role of Transportation in Regional Economic Development,* A Charles Rivers Associates Research Study (Lexington, Mass., 1971), pp. 69-72.
34. Quoted in Saint John *Standard,* 7 June 1921.

35. Evidence, B.R.C., 1926, p. 6602, and Henry et al., *Railway Freight Rates,* pp. 266-68.
36. "Exhibits presented to the Commission at Halifax and Saint John, January 17-19", Evidence, B.R.C., 1922; see especially pp. 7, 22-24, and 32-34.
37. The Dominion Iron and Steel Corporation entered receivership in 1926 and its receiver subsequently began legal action to "wind up" the parent corporation. Halifax *Herald,* 2 July 1926, and 2 April 1927.
38. *Busy East of Canada* (Sackville), February 1921, and Evidence, B.R.C., 1922, p. 496.
39. *Debates,* 1920, p. 2566.
40. Evidence, Royal Commission on Maritime Claims, 1926, pp. 2031-37.
41. *Canada Year Book,* 1929, p. 401.
42. Employed in manufacturing:

	1920	1926
Amherst	2,267	735
Dartmouth	1,581	946
Halifax	7,171	3,287
New Glasgow	2,610	611
Sydney	2,929	2,053
Truro	1,080	778
Moncton	3,061	2,133
Saint John	4,630	3,394

SOURCE: Ibid., 1922-23, p. 438, and 1929, pp. 453-54.

43. Dominion Bureau of Statistics, *The Maritime Provinces in their Relation to the National Economy* (Ottawa, 1948), p. 10.
44. Calculated from departmental reports and "Railway Statistics," 1917-22. See especially *Sessional Papers,* 1921, No. 20, pp. 87-88 and 1922, No. 20, p. 105. Since after 1920 the railway revealed only the value rather than actual volume of traffic carried, the amount given for the decline in traffic can only be a rough approximation. Unfortunately, for the purposes of this study, the detailed statistical analyses of the Intercolonial's traffic, revenue, and expenditures, prepared initially by the department and later by the Dominion Bureau of Statistics, terminated in 1921.
45. D.B. Hanna attributed the deficits of the C.N.R. as a whole to more efficient bookkeeping procedures which charged "all possible costs" to the operating account; Hanna, *Trains of Recollection,* p. 278. Recorded capital expenditures on the Intercolonial were sharply reduced in the early 1920s. Whether this was a result of greater honesty in accounting or merely the neglect of the lines in question is not clear. Certainly Hanna's successors showed no hesitation in charging to capital expenditures elsewhere in the system. The capital account for the C.N.R. increased by a total of $456 million between 1923 and 1931; Henry, *Railway Freight Rates,* p. 23.
46. Evidence, B.R.C., 1926, pp. 6635 and 6889-90.
47. Meighen to G.F. Buskard, 8 October 1921, and Buskard to Meighen, 9

October 1921, Arthur Meighen Papers, P.A.C.; *L'Evangeline* (Moncton), 13 October 1921.

48. Halifax *Morning Chronicle,* 16 November 1921; see also Halifax *Herald,* 25 September 1921.

49. W.L.M. King Diaries, 1 February 1922, P.A.C.

50. Quoted in *Debates,* 1922, p. 355.

51. Evidence, B.R.C., 1926, p. 6927.

52. See E.R. Forbes "The Maritime Rights Movement, 1919-1927: A Study in Canadian Regionalism" (PH.D. thesis, Queen's University, 1975), chaps. 5 and 7.

53. *Report of the Royal Commission on Maritime Claims* (Ottawa, 1926), pp. 22-26.

54. Evidence, Royal Commission on Maritime Claims, pp. 2205-10.

55. Halifax *Morning Chronicle,* 31 August 1926.

56. Toronto *Globe,* 28 January 1927.

57. "Visit of Commissioner to Ottawa. February 3-8, 1927," Minutes of the Saint John Board of Trade, New Brunswick Museum.

58. See W.L.M. King Diaries, 15 and 18 March, P.A.C. In outlining the government's response to the Report in Parliament, King skillfully glossed over or ignored all elements of the Report rejected by the cabinet and claimed that the government's proposed program represented the implementation of the commission's recommendations "virtually in their entirety." *Debates,* 1926-27, pp. 1334-37.

59. In the ten-class rate system, first-class rates were exactly double those of fifth class, Henry, *Railway Freight Rates,* p. 85.

60. *Canadian Rate Cases,* Vol. 44, p. 289, and Vol. 46, p. 161. For a useful survey of B.R.C. decisions and Royal Commission recommendations as they pertained to the Maritimes after 1927, see Maritime Transportation Commission, *Submission to the Royal Commission on Transportation, 1960;* hereafter cited as M.T.C. *Submission.*

61. *Report of the Royal Commission on Transportation* (Ottawa, 1951), p. 236.

62. M.T.C. *Submission,* Vol. 1, p. 22.

63. Ibid., Vol. II, Appendix IV, and The Economist Intelligence Unit, *Atlantic Provinces Transportation Study,* Vol. V, (Ottawa, 1967), p. 22.

64. The Economist Intelligence Unit, ibid., pp. 23-24 and 30-31.

65. M.T.C. *Submission,* Vol. II, Appendix V.

66. *Final Report of the Royal Commission on Canada's Economic Prospects* (Ottawa, 1957), p. 408.

67. *Royal Commission on Transportation* (Ottawa, 1961), Vol. II, pp. 109-12.

68. The Economist Intelligence Unit, *Atlantic Provinces Transportation Study,* Vol. IV, passim.

69. Atlantic Premiers, *The Basic Elements of an Atlantic Provinces Transportation Policy,* 1969, pp. 11-14.

70. See "Third Report of the Federal-Provincial Commitee on Atlantic Region Transportation," 1973, Appendix I.

71. Atlantic Provinces Transportation Commission, *Transportation Review and*

Annual Report, 1973-1974, pp. 21-23.

72. See Saint John *Telegraph-Journal,* 23 January 1975.
73. Toronto *Globe and Mail,* 17 January 1975.
74. See H.J. Darling, "Transport Policy in Canada: The Struggle of Ideologies Versus Realities," *Issues in Canadian Transport Policy,* ed. K.W. Studnicki-Gizbert (Toronto, 1974), p.9.
75. M.T.C. *Submission,* p. 43.
76. J.C.R. Hanley, "The Railway Industry," Transportation and the Atlantic Region. A symposium sponsored by the Roads and Transportation Association of Canada, Moncton, 22-23 April 1974, pp. 123-24.

T. W. ACHESON

The Maritimes and "Empire Canada"

Few themes have been more persistent in Canadian history than the characterization of Canada—and British North America before it—as an "open" society, open in the sense that its economic life has been dominated by a continuous inward and outward flow of people, enterprise, commodities, and capital on a scale rarely matched elsewhere in the modern world. The effect of this experience has been reflected in the metropolitan tradition which has dominated the writing of Canadian history for more than a generation. Sometimes appearing in the guise of a staples theory, sometimes stated in the more complex political-economic form of Laurentianism, and more recently evident as a broad social theory of metropolitanism, this tradition largely rests upon the assumption of an open society and of the nature of the relationships which bound British North America to other societies and political jurisdictions.

In the pre-Confederation era the stimulus for economic change or expansion typically occurred outside British North American society. At its worst, the system reduced the colonial economies to a state of utter dependence on the metropolitan economy; at the same time, a strong and vital metropolitan economy could confer both inestimable economic benefits and a sense of place and status upon its client. All of the British North American colonies, and particularly those on the Atlantic seaboard, experienced both elements of this patron–client relationship.

Central to this pre-Confederation experience was the persistent British migration into the North American colonies, a migration so extensive that significant changes were effected in the demographic characteristics of colonial society in almost every decade of the nineteenth century.[1] At times, in mid-century it is probable that an absolute majority of adult English-speaking inhabitants of British North America had been born in the British Isles. Nor was this migration drawn largely from among labourers and tenants. The groups which arrived in British North America may not have comprehended every element within the several British social systems, but they did contain a broad cross-section. Merchants, lawyers, placemen, and retired military officers mingled with English freeholders, Irish mechanics, and Scottish crofters in search of new fields of exploitation. Even in the Maritime provinces, where population growth was slower and the native-born composed a larger segment of the population than was the case in the upper provinces, British migrants probably comprised at least 20 per cent of the adult population at any time before Confederation and in many areas of the region were, at times, even more significant.[2] These migrants included a substantial number of businessmen anxious to exploit the colonial resources, and an even larger number of artisans and mechanics who laid the foundations for much of the technology of the colonies. As early as 1812, the business communities of Saint John and Halifax were dominated by dozens of Scottish merchants, most of whom had come to the colonies as young men, sometimes as agents of Scottish firms but more often as men of some means and commercial experience seeking out new opportunities.[3] While the proportion of native entrepreneurs certainly rose as the century progressed, the presence of a large number of immigrant businessmen—particularly among the great merchants who dominated the shipping trades—became a permanent feature of the Maritime business community.

Whether businessmen or not, immigrants generally were welcomed as agents of development by colonial leaders. The most notable exception to this rule was the influx of Irish fleeing the famines of the 1840s, an event which placed severe strains on the meagre social service agencies of the lower provinces. But most migrants brought with them needed skills and capital. The arrival of 1,000 such families in any given year would provide a significant stimulus to the economies of colonies like Nova Scotia or New Brunswick where total annual provincial revenues rarely reached £100,000 before 1840.

The movement of capital into the colonies by means of migrants was only part of the picture. Aside from social capital for major public works, which was raised in British North America as in the United States on the British money market, the Maritime economy experienced a persistent flow of capital into the region in conjunction with the exploitation of natural resources. The New Brunswick woods industry is a case in point. The story of the rapid expansion of the timber trade as a result of political and fiscal decisions made at the height of the Napoleonic wars, and the impact of this development upon the colonial societies, is well known. Less well known is the development of the masting trade of the 1790s which in turn stimulated the colonial shipbuilding industry. The capital and technology required for both of these activities was supplied mainly from Scotland through the medium of firms such as those of John and William Black and Christopher Scott.[4] The role of the British entrepreneur in the New Brunswick timber trade reached its zenith in the 1830s and 1840s with the development of the Rankine empire on the Miramichi. But the traditions persisted long after the fall of the old colonial economic system. As late as the 1800s the Belfast firm of Stewart Bros. remained one of the three great lumber firms of the province and its collapse in 1887 brought down the Maritime Bank, the second largest financial institution in New Brunswick.[5]

By the 1830s an increasing interest was being taken in the province's timber resources by Boston and New York interests[6] anxious to acquire new sources in the face of failing woods supplies along the American Atlantic coast. Although this investment declined following the recession of 1837, it re-asserted itself after 1850 and became a significant element in the woods industry of the St. Croix and Saint John river valleys.[7]

In addition to capital investment and technical skills, the

economic relationship between the Maritime colonies and the motherland permitted the development of a significant merchant marine together with a number of supporting financial institutions. The shipping industry grew rapidly; at its height in the 1860s it ranked fourth among the merchant marines of the world. The colonial financial system which it produced included not only a dozen banks, among which were the two most stable financial institutions in British North America, but also numerous marine and other insurance companies which played leading roles in the economy of the region. The value of these secondary benefits is revealed in the 1841 Saint John Board of Trade report which estimated that the freights earned by New Brunswick vessels amounted to £334,000 that year—a sum which compared favourably with the £639,000 worth of exports shipped from the province.[8]

Of even greater importance to the whole economic system which linked the British Isles and the Maritime provinces in the first half of the nineteenth century was the British imperial market, which was capable of consuming virtually the entire output of the colonies' staples industries. There were periodic breakdowns in the system—notably in the mid-1820s and early 1840s—but on the whole it made possible a higher standard of living in most staples-producing areas than would have been the case if the colonies had been less specialized in their production. Virtually all squared timber and deals and most ships and dried and salted fish were exported. Normally about two-thirds of the woods products and half of the fish were sold on the British market and about half the remainder of both staples were disposed of in the British West Indies. Even in the decades following the dismantling of the mercantilist system, most Maritime woods products, ships, and fish were marketed in the United Kingdom and the British West Indies. Most of the remaining output was sold in the United States where the depletion of the woods resources along the American east coast led to a steadily increasing demand for Maritime deals and lumber in that market by mid-century. This pattern of distribution characterized most Maritime resource industries until the First World War.

The Confederation of the Maritimes and the Canadas had little effect on these trading patterns. The dominance of the economic assumptions of the staples producers was reflected in the early economic policies of the union which emphasized revenue tariffs, free trade, and the development of international markets.[9] This is not to suggest that there was no opposition to those assumptions. Every major urban centre in the country possessed a growing and influential middle class of industrialists, artisans, and their proletarian allies who demanded a more dynamic role on the part of government in the development of secondary industry in Canada. For the moment this growing army of secondary producers could only agitate against the older tradition; their day had to await the collapse of the old order. That crisis occurred in the depression of 1874-79, when the British and American markets for Canadian woods products and grains experienced a sharp downturn. To further aggravate the situation many American businessmen, faced with contracting domestic markets, began dumping large quantities of manufactured products on the Canadian market at substantially reduced prices. The combination of failing markets and foreign competition drove hundreds of manufacturers into bankruptcy and seemed to threaten the very survival of the small and comparatively inefficient Canadian manufacturing sector. Fearing the consequences for the economy of a continued downturn, a substantial portion of the commercial community came to advocate national fiscal policies of protection by 1878.[10]

In the face of this crisis the governments of Mackenzie and Macdonald turned to the ideology of the protectionists. That ideology was militantly nationalist; its models the British, German, and American industrial economies. The ideal of nationhood was a self-sufficient economy with the industrial potential to provide, if necessary, all basic manufactured products. Above all, the hallmark of a modern nation was its ability to produce limitless quantities of steel and iron.[11] A people beset by economic difficulties clutched at this ideology, and its rhetoric captured a significant part of the public imagination. The nation emerged from its worst economic difficulties by 1900, but by then the ideal of national economic self-sufficiency and of an economy which could be controlled internally had joined the myths of a national railway and banking institutions as a basic requirement of nationhood.

Under the circumstances, the acceptance of this premise by Canadian political leaders of both parties is understandable. The desire to create a strong independent national economy, both in emulation of the American experience and out of fear that failure to follow the American example would result in the submersion of the Canadian nationality, was a powerful motive. This defensive nationalism, as Hugh Aitken has termed it,[12] was reflected not only in the forced development of a Canadian industrial potential, but also in the too rapid westward expansion of the Canadian state and the subsequent construction of the Canadian Pacific Railway.

The combination of fiscal policies adopted by the Macdonald government between 1879 and 1887, commonly referred to as the National Policy, was designed to protect every important economic interest in the country and to integrate the diverse regional economies of the new state into a relatively self-sufficient national economy. To achieve these ends protection was provided to primary as well as secondary producers. Nova Scotia coal was to be forced into Montreal and even to Toronto, while the product of the Simcoe wheat fields was to replace that of Pennsylvania on Maritime tables. But the truly radical elements in the policy centred on secondary industry. Initially the tariff attempted to protect and promote the expansion of a number of existing manufacturing industries and the employment opportunities which they provided. Happily, the introduction of the National Policy coincided with an upswing in international demand for Canadian produce to permit a rapid industrial expansion. As this initial momentum slowed after 1882, the government attempted to stimulate it again by broadening the tariff base. To this end tariff policy became an instrument to force development in a number of manufacturing industries many of which had either not existed before 1880 or existed in only a very limited form. [13] To many observers of the period it seemed obvious that continued support of such a range of significant industries was going to remake the Canadian economy and would create a situation in which the government which had promoted the new order would find itself morally bound to preserve it.

In many ways, these observers were right. Each new firm created under the aegis of "national" policy strengthened the hands of the protectionists. As well, while these policies of national development did not actually compare with the traditional staples interests, they clearly encouraged the diversion of skills, capital, and other resources from them into the development of the new enterprises. The energies of Canadians were to be devoted more and more to the production of goods for domestic consumption as the National Policy increasingly fulfilled its promise of making the entire domestic market available to Canadian producers. Thus, in reaction to the problems of an international economy which was unable to consume Canadian staples, and in response to the demands of a variety of concerned business interests, the Canadian government moved to restore the traditional metropolis–hinterland economic relationships that had sustained the Maritime economy for more than a century.

The perspective of most Maritime entrepreneurs to the new order was quite different from that of their Montreal or Toronto counterparts. The effect of the reorganization was to create a new economic metropolis, centred on Montreal, replacing the traditional British and American centres. The Maritimes had long been a region of powerful external metropolises and weak internal ones. Saint John had been the most successful of the latter, dominating the commerce of the Bay of Fundy drainage basin, but, despite numerous efforts, the city never had been able to play a significant role on the north shore of its own province. Indeed most Maritime entrepreneurs were unabashed colonials. They had been raised in a political and social milieu which had emphasized this status and even endowed it with a certain mystique and prestige. To be a junior partner in a relationship where the senior was one of the most universally respected states in the world never had been deemed servility by an elite which gloried in being British.

The transition to the new order was not accomplished easily by such an elite. A tradition of three generations' standing provided a powerful psychological barrier to its acceptance. Even in decline, the woods and fishing industries remained the backbone of the regional economy and part of a commercial system through which most leading entrepreneurs had achieved their wealth and status. Yet many Maritime leaders recognized the possibilities of an industrial order in which the Maritimes, surrounded by the Canadas, the American east coast, and Europe, and possessing the only significant supplies of Canadian coal, might well play some significant role. In the old shipbuilding and decaying staples country of peninsular Nova Scotia and the Bay of Fundy drainage basin of New Brunswick, staples entrepreneurs joined small-scale local secondary manufacturers in an effort to revive the flagging fortunes of numerous towns and cities whose prosperity had been built on the production and distribution of woods products and fish.[14] The decade of the 1880s witnessed a rapid development of secondary industry in these communities. The value of the output of cotton and sugar mills, rope, confectionery, and glass factories, and secondary iron and steel manufacturing plants together surpassed that of the sawmill, and while the latter remained the largest industrial employer in the region, the average annual income of workers in the new industries was often twice as large as that in the wood-processing industries.[15] This development was aided greatly by the reorganization of the vehicles of regional commerce: the transport of coal by sea to Montreal became the principal employment of the Nova Scotian merchant marine, while the Intercolonial and Short Line railroads firmly fastened the region to Montreal and gradually eroded the traditional seaborne import trade of the Maritimes. Momentarily it seemed as if the transition from the British to the Canadian metropolis could be accomplished with a minimum of social disruption.

Yet it soon became apparent that the Canadian metropolis was unable to perform most of the functions usually associated with a dominant centre. Since Canadians apparently preferred sugar and cottons to lumber, the Maritime entrepreneurs built cotton mills and sugar refineries and produced sugar and cloth. But these industries were developed by Maritimers with technical assistance from Europe and America; capital was raised locally or in America and Great Britain. Even the largest Nova Scotian coal, iron, and steel firms were of local or American

foundation. The most critical metropolitan failure was the inability of the Central Canadian market to consume the output of
these new regional industries. Overproduction and fierce price
wars in many industries brought about the first attempts to control the output of various industries in the late 1880s and early
1890s, and these efforts culminated in the horizontal consolidation of many new Maritime industries which were henceforth
controlled from Montreal or Toronto. A second wave of con-
solidations—in the early twentieth century—completed this
process and resulted in control of most Maritime secondary
industry by entrepreneurs and corporations in Central
Canada.[16] Frequently, in their zeal to acquire control of all producing elements within an industry, some of the consolidated
companies engaged in fierce price wars, deliberately dumping
into the Maritime market in an effort to drive their small
regional competitors into consolidation or bankruptcy. By 1914
the Maritimes had become a branch-plant economy.

The consolidation movement in the industrial sectors of the
regional economy was paralleled in the financial. Between 1900
and 1920 every component in the century-old Maritime banking system was swept away and replaced by branches of great
national banking consortia. The banks of New Brunswick and
Nova Scotia, the two most stable and conservative financial
institutions in the Dominion, were amalgamated, along with the
Metropolitan Bank and the Bank of Ottawa into the Bank of
Nova Scotia, effective ownership and control of which passed
to the Central Canadian shareholders. The Halifax Banking
Company was absorbed by the Bank of Commerce in 1903, the
Peoples Bank of Halifax by the Bank of Montreal in 1905, and
the Union Bank of Halifax by the Royal Bank of Canada in
1910.[17]

In many respects this rationalization of industry, banking,
and railways was a necessary pre-condition for the protection
and development of a viable Canadian economy. Once the
value and necessity of a comprehensive national economy
based on the Laurentian system and capable of some reasonable degree of industrial self-sufficiency was accepted, the spo-
liation of much of the Maritime industrial capacity became an
unfortunate necessity undertaken in the name of economic

efficiency. Yet there is little evidence to suggest that most Maritime industries were not at least as efficient as that of their central Canadian counterparts,[18] nor, given advantageous freight rates, that they could not compete for most central Canadian markets. Latter-day claims by consolidated corporations—such as the cottons firms and the successors to Dominion and Nova Scotia Steel and Coal—that Maritime plants were obsolescent are difficult to evaluate because much of this obsolescence was the result of management decisions made after the mergers.

By 1914 the National Policy had achieved its ends both in the Maritimes and in the Montreal heartland. While the years following the First World War witnessed some marginal extensions of the policy into areas of new technology, these were granted generally as relief to multinational corporations. The major areas of Canadian control within the Canadian industrial economy remained those that had been protected and developed before 1914. Even then the policies of national industrial development had not provided sufficient employment to offset the decline in agriculture, the staples industries, and the ancient urban trades such as clothing and footwear. The result was a steady emigration from the region. In the interwar years, as these consolidated corporations began to close out their Maritime branches and to concentrate their production facilities in Central Canada, the exodus continued and was coupled with a relative decline in the region's per-capita income in comparison with the rest of the country.[19]

The most depressing element in this sequence of events was that the region was being turned rapidly into a client economy, incapable of producing goods for consumption in the Central Canadian market, yet forced by the very national policies that had earlier promised economic security to supply most of its consumers' needs from Central Canadian industry. The result by the 1920s was a stagnant debtor economy with a declining industrial sector. Having provided the instrument through which most of the Maritime secondary industry had been built, the National Policy and its masters—perhaps reflecting the new political realities—were unable to provide the kinds of modifications which might have preserved and further stimulated the industrial potential of the region. Instead, the rigidities of the original policies were institutionalized into a permanent tariff system while the flexible elements within them—such as differential freight rates and protection for a variety of specialized regional commodities—which might have comprehended and compensated for the needs of special groups and interests within the national framework, were gradually abandoned.

The national policies had been designed to protect the economic interests of Canadians, to provide opportunities for employment, and to develop a relatively self-sufficient Canadian economy. If they were unable in the long run to protect the interests of regions or groups, it might be expected that they at least would create national centres to which ambitious or desperate Maritimers could emigrate without prejudice. Not even this benefit accrued to the region. During the first three decades of the twentieth century at least 300,000 Maritime natives abandoned the region.[20] Only a small proportion of these settled in Central and Western Canada: the 1931 census found just 21,000 Maritimers in all Ontario, considerably fewer in Quebec, and only a slightly larger number on the Prairies and in British Columbia.[21] All evidence would seem to indicate that at least three-quarters of migrants followed the traditional route to the United States. And that migration was a morale-destroying experience which saw most Maritime communities bereft of the greater part of their most productive people. Perhaps half of the population which came to adulthood during this period migrated from the region and this element almost certainly contained more than half of the region's high school graduates and those possessing technical and other skills. Significantly, nearly half of the emigration of the whole period occurred between 1921 and 1931.

Left to its own devices the process of de-industrialization would have produced a rapidly declining economy and population in the interwar years. Production and employment in Maritime manufacturing industry fell by nearly 40 per cent between 1917 and 1921. Yet, by 1929 it had recovered to more than 75 per cent of the 1971 levels.[22]

The key to this conundrum was the revival of the staples industries and a dramatic resurgence of the Maritimes' traditional markets in the United Kingdom and the United States.

The manufacture of lumber had remained an important but largely static element in the regional economy until the First World War. After 1900 this activity was supplemented by the development of the new pulp and paper technology. It was a slow development: from three plants producing $108,000 worth of pulp in 1880, to twelve plants and $1,400,000 in 1911.[23] By the latter date, however, the foundations had been forged and in the immediate postwar period a rapid transition was made to the manufacture of paper. By 1930 an industry capitalized at $64,000,000, employing more than 3,000 men and producing pulp and paper to the annual value of $17,000,000 had been created, exceeding in all categories even the declining pig-iron, steel, and rolled-products industries of Nova Scotia.[24] A number of local entrepreneurs such as the Fraser family in the upper Saint John River valley and the Dickies in Nova Scotia played a role in the early development of this new staple, but it was American corporate enterprise, such as the International Paper Company, and American capital that played the major role in this development. Equally important, it was the American economy which absorbed most of its output.[25]

After the First World War these two tendencies—the decline of the consumer goods sectors and the expansion of staples output—became more pronounced. During the interwar period the output of goods destined for domestic markets continued their steady downslide as machine shops, cotton mills, car factories, secondary iron and steel products mills, chemical products factories, and numerous other Maritime plants were either transferred to Central Canada, closed out by parent organizations in Central Canada, or forced into bankruptcy by the draconian freight-rates policies adopted by the Canadian National Railway system.[26] As well, the region was rapidly becoming the victim of a technological shift which saw the industrial emphasis on coal and iron replaced by one based upon hydro-electric power and chemicals.[27] And the decline of Canadian railway construction in the 1920s was reflected in the Nova Scotia steel industry. Parallelling this decline was a continuous rise in the value and variety of imports of manufactured goods from Central Canada to supply the Maritime domestic market. These ranged from the products of a sophisticated technology such as that of the new automobile industry to those of such simple and labour-intensive technologies as the needle trades. Indeed it was the import of the latter that produced the most devastating effect on the Maritime economy. Traditional mass-consumption industries such as the clothing trades are the largest employer in any major urban centre. The Maritime cities had been no exception to this rule in the late nineteenth century; yet, where there had been more than 6,700 seamstresses and tailors in the region in 1880, there were only 1,600 some fifty years later.[28] A similar decline could be noted in most basic consumer-good industries. At the same time the processing of the staples, lumber, pulp, and fish, rapidly became an even more important element in the region's manufacturing sector, the value of output rising from about 32 per cent of all manufactures in 1911 to 38 per cent in 1951.[29]

Curiously, the very success of the new staples development placed still greater strains on an already fragmented regional society. Its effect was to shift the industrial geography of the region from one of relative concentration in a dozen communities of eastern Nova Scotia and southern New Brunswick to a diffusion scattered around the perimeters of the region. The result was to nourish the various subregional particularisms within the region, to strengthen a number of small scattered centres, and at the same time to permit the already seriously weakened regional metropolises like Halifax and Saint John to experience a still further decline. Montreal and Toronto had undergone a similar experience with the opening of the resource areas of Quebec and Ontario, but the latter became important additions to the commercial and financial empires of the traditional metropolises which were able to become the major service centres to the new regions and thus reap a double increment from their prosperity both as suppliers of consumer goods manufactured in the cities and of financial and other services. The Maritime cities could be neither. As vestiges of the mid-nineteenth-century staples economy reasserted themselves, the sea routes linking the producer directly to the consumer were reestablished. While Halifax and Saint John businessmen would often act as distributors of consumer goods to these communities the goods were rarely produced in the region. Moreover as national merchandising firms became more prominent after the Second World War even this function was frequently usurped as goods were distributed either directly from Montreal or through special regional depots.

And step by step, as this process continued, the Maritime economy was becoming more and more alienated from the national. By 1950 most exported Maritime-manufactured output was being sold on foreign markets,[30] something which had not occurred before in a century and a half. In effect the region derived only marginal benefits from the national economic policies; virtually any monetary benefits derived from the region's staples economy in the form of wages or capital expansion were spent in the Canadian market largely for Central Canadian products, most of which were purchased at a considerable premium over comparable American goods. Any metropolis-hinterland relation implies some terms of reciprocity and mutual benefit. As an economic metropolis the Central Canadian centres had failed their Maritime hinterland; by mid-century the Central Canadian position had become largely exploitative.

Given the distribution of population and resources, was not this development inevitable? Would not any attempt to maintain or develop a substantial secondary manufacturing sector in the Maritimes have created an inefficient and costly albatross, a perpetual burden on the Canadian nation? Examination of any of the primers on the Canadian economy written in the mid-twentieth century reveals that most commentators were prepared to place the stamp of "inevitability" on the situation. In such a view the de-industrialization of the Maritimes was natural and therefore "right." The means through which it was accomplished were irrelevant; a similar end would have been achieved by any other path.

Certainly it would be difficult to defend the maintenance of a regional industrial system in which the level of productivity was substantially lower than that in other parts of the country. Yet, despite the assumption that such differences did exist, there is little evidence to support the argument. Indeed the most recent study of the subject in Nova Scotia indicates that existing industry is quite capable of competing with its Central Canadian counterparts,[31] an impression that is given as well in any examination of Maritime industry in the 1880s and 1920s. Roy E. George has found, for example, that benefits enjoyed by

Central Canadian industry as a result of economies of scale have been exaggerated, while somewhat lower wages in the Maritimes help to offset Central Canadian advantages. He concluded that the significant differences in industrial performance between the two regions (Nova Scotia and Central Canada) were the result of an inferior entrepreneurship in the former.

If this is so we are into the realm of complex cultural factors. Certainly much of the industrial failure has resulted from weaknesses within regional society: if Maritime firms were purchased and then closed by their Central Canadian competitors, they were certainly sold by Maritime businessmen and shareholders either over-willing to take an immediate profit or too fearful of the consequences of a protracted trade war with their larger adversaries. This conservatism has long been a feature of regional business life but does reflect the historical realities. Such traits and values are conditioned from generations of experience and expectation. In 1867 Canada had assumed control of a fragile society, one with a long colonial social tradition, and with a small and recently emancipated bourgeoisie only beginning to develop a consciousness of itself and the possibilities of its society. Aside from the initial industrial thrust in the generation following 1880, this bourgeoisie had never been given the opportunity to develop or expand. If French Canada suffered a form of social decapitation in the mid-eighteenth century, Maritime societies have suffered a similar fate in every generation since the First World War. The oft-painted picture of a long-established conservative business elite in the Maritimes has been overly used; the principal characteristic of the society has been the lack of a powerful self-directed and self-confident business community. The insecurity of twentieth-century Maritime business life has tended to produce two kinds of men: those marginal and insecure figures, always fearful of failure, who were prepared to eke out a living on the periphery of Canadian business life without committing themselves to any substantial enterprise; and the socially irresponsible opportunist rapaciously streaking his way across the limited Maritime firmament in a desperate attempt to "succeed" before the failure struck. In either case they reflected the colonial attitudes and the ingrained insecurities of their society. Exceptions to these stereotypes—and there have been some in each generation—tend to stand out against a barren landscape. They were relatively few in number and lacked a substantial middle-class milieu in which to operate. The region possessed no large urban conglomeration which could act as a focus for their economic and social activities. Despite the bright promises of the National Policy, no major dynamic centres emerged in the Maritimes in which a bourgeoisie could be nurtured and a regional tradition fostered. Instead stagnation, emigration, and de-industrialization thwarted, then destroyed, much of the potential which the region possessed in the last quarter of the nineteenth century.

Given the assumptions and political realities of early twentieth-century Canadian life and the fragile character of Maritime society the experience of de-industrialization was probably "inevitable." Yet the effects of the "natural law" of industrial centralization and consolidation could have been mitigated by political intervention with only a marginal decline in national living standards. And the concept of a quid pro quo, of the need to defend all interests, was something well understood and clearly expressed by the original framers of the National Policy. The alternative to it was the creation of a special "Maritime Problem," clearly evident by the 1920s, which was to become the object of national study, debate, and political action throughout mid-century. Two interrelated solutions to the problem have been advocated. One was to accelerate the process of emigration, abandon the region as an area of significant settlement, and gradually absorb most of the population into other parts of the national community. The second was to raise the quality of life in the region by means of transfer payments, at first to individuals, later to institutions, in the hope that national social policies would succeed where economic policies had failed.

The introduction of a number of social-service programs in the 1940s and 1950s did much to soften the economic downturn occasioned by the phasing out of the war economy and to prevent a further relative decline in the living standards of the region. The programs were initiated by transfer payments to individuals in the form of unemployment insurance, children's allowances, and old-age pensions, all designed to provide minimum living standards to economically vulnerable portions of the community. These were augmented in the 1950s by federal-provincial cost-sharing agreements designed to permit institutions such as hospitals and colleges to maintain a standard level of services across the nation. Finally, beginning in 1957, a comprehensive program of equalization payments was initiated. This was done to provide the poorer provinces with lump-sum payments which could be used to maintain reasonable standards of public service.

Roy George has estimated that by 1962 about 8 per cent of the personal incomes of Nova Scotians was composed of federal transfer payments;[32] by 1972 transfer payments for social purposes may well have exceeded 10 per cent of personal income in the region while federal installations, such as armed forces bases, may have accounted for another 7 or 8 per cent.[33] The social policies of national development had achieved their purposes. In the two decades following the war the worst sores of poverty within the region were treated, certain basic social institutions were strengthened—if young Maritimers continued to emigrate, at least many arrived in the metropolitan centres of Quebec and Ontario with some basic skills—and the region was transformed into the most centralized and integrated part of the Canadian social order.

These victories were bought at a heavy price. In the course of achieving them, the Maritime provinces were transformed into client states of the federal government. The colonialism was far more totalitarian in concept and effectiveness than the unwieldly British system had been. Two deleterious results of the policy were quickly evident. In the first place there was a dramatic growth in the labour force during the 1960s, but most of this growth occurred in the service sector as thousands sought niches of security in the extensive civil-service structures which were erected to administer the new social programs. Always a most important component in the regional economy, the provincial governments replaced even the combined woods industries as the largest regional industry in the 1960s.[34] By 1970 a far larger proportion of Maritime workers were in the service industries than was the case in any other part of the nation, and the proportion appeared to be rising.[35] As it did, productivity fell. Over-all, there were proportionally more civil servants, more academics, and more teachers in the Maritimes than any other part of the nation.

The psychological impact of the new policies was much more subtle. The bonuses provided by the new social policies permitted the breakdown of many conventions and structures, some of which had already ceased to perform any meaningful social function. They also permitted the combining of some of the most undesirable features of the older systems with the new affluence to produce an even more difficult situation. Notable among these was a loss of initiative, one which saw the Maritimes drawn into an ever-enlarging web of dependence. The impact of this phenomenon was particularly noticeable in rural areas. Between 1950 and 1970 the region was transformed from a predominantly rural economy of marginal but productive farms to a rural society of non-productive farms, the inhabitants of which derived their livelihood from a combination of government benefits, wages from urban service occupations, and seasonal income from the woods industries. By 1970 the principal rural society in Canada was not even self-sufficient in the most basic agricultural commodities.

Another side effect of the federal intervention was the creation of a new bourgeoisie elite composed of professional civil servants, medical doctors, and academics who joined the traditional lawyer-politician-businessman leadership of the community and gave to it a distinctly professional flavour. Indeed, with its emphasis upon place and sinecures, and with the patron-client relationship which the monopolistic hierarchies of provincial governments and institutions of higher learning encouraged, Maritime society began more closely to resemble an eighteenth- than a nineteenth-century society. In this social structure the medical doctor became the principal and wealthiest entrepreneur, and the lawyer—in his quest of the role of power-broker—the greatest of speculators. But it was a captive elite largely dependent for opportunity, position, and status on federal resources and ultimately subject to the will of the federal government. Most important, it was an elite with no resource base, one incapable of generating anything more than services; producers of primary or secondary goods played little role in its ranks.

In one sense the search for industry never ceased in the Maritimes, not even in the nadir of the 1920s and 1930s. As late as the 1960s community organizations and municipal governments throughout the Maritimes vied with each other for the limited and decreasing numbers of manufacturing industries in a manner reminiscent of Ontario communities in the 1890s. This was done by a series of subsidies through which a substantial part of the operating and capital costs of an enterprise were borne by the community as a whole and were donated to the entrepreneur. The commonest form of subsidy was relief from municipal or school taxes for a period of years or in perpetuity. In addition, many communities provided free land, free serviced lots, free and unlimited quantities of municipal water; others made forgiveable capital gifts or purchased "stock" in the enterprise. In the case of larger firms such subsidies were made only at considerable continuing cost to the communities, and the owners of such firms were not above forcing further concessions out of the municipalities by threats of leaving for another community.

Within the resource sector the activities of the provinces parallelled those of their municipalities. Control of coal and timberlands always had been used by the governments of Nova Scotia and New Brunswick as a vehicle to create a greater industrial potential within their provincial borders. Until the Second World War the slender financial resources of the provincial governments, coupled with their responsibilities for education, health, welfare, and basic transportation facilities, made any comprehensive program of industrial development an impossibility.[36] Lack of resources prevented even an adequate commitment of social capital to build the modern highways, ports, facilities, electric power sources, and other infrastructure needed for the promotion of an industrial state.

The movement of federal resources into these traditional spheres of provincial responsibility materially assisted the hard-pressed governments and enabled them to offer more extensive incentives for economic growth. One of the earliest signs of this new emphasis was the creation in 1954 of the Atlantic Provinces Economic Council—a research and advisory body organized by the Atlantic Provinces Board of Trade which was designed to monitor the regional economy. In the late 1950s both the Nova Scotia and New Brunswick governments created Crown corporations—Industrial Estates and New Brunswick Development Corporation—possessing statutory authority to produce and implement comprehensive programs of industrial development and to stimulate this growth by provincial loans or grants to appropriate entrepreneurs. In 1965 Prince Edward Island organized Industrial Enterprises Incorporated which was modelled on Industrial Estates. These corporations possessed the authority to provide capital for industrial development raised on the provincial credit and to become creditors and co-owners of private concerns. These developments were stimulated further by the federal government's efforts to cope with the problem of regional discrepancy. Until 1960 this was done largely through fiscal equalization policies. After that time an attempt was made by the Diefenbaker government to deal with specific problems by direct federal intervention into the Maritime economy. This resulted in the creation of the Agricultural and Rural Development Programme in 1961, the Atlantic Development Board in 1962, and the Area Development Programme industrial incentives in 1963. Finally, in 1969, in an effort to create the framework for a comprehensive development program, the Trudeau government created the Department of Regional Economic Expansion.[37]

With the exception of the D.R.E.E. programs most decisions of these various development agencies were made within the region. Many of these decisions involved the development of schools, colleges, transportation networks, utilities, energy supplies, and other infrastructure needed to support the industrial goals of the regional leaders. Many others involved direct aid to private firms both inside and outside the region, and incentives to entrepreneurs to initiate new enterprises. The strategies for this development have ranged from a crude scattergun approach of offering assistance to all comers to more selective concepts. These include the growth-centre technique, designed to focus development in several specified communities, and an emphasis upon sophisticated light-weight technology (such as electronics) to overcome the problems of transportation costs to markets far away.

Of all public issues in the Maritimes, few have provoked as much discussion as has the direct subsidization of private firms. Reasons for the controversy abound. The history of much of this development has been marked by the ghosts of numerous failures: like the scriptural sower, the development agencies have cast much seed for little return in the hope that those kernels that survive will yield the economic salvation of the region. And to the high failure rate is added the further indictment of many Central Canadians that much of the development represents a robbing of the Ontario Peter to pay the Maritime Paul as branches of international firms enticed by the handsome relocation benefits abandon Central Canadian centres.

Despite these charges, despite the weaknesses of the granting agencies and the venality of many of the recipients, the development programs represent the first serious attempt to reintegrate the region into a national economy in more than half a century. As such they start a long way back and have a great distance to go. Economically this means the re-industrialization of the Maritimes. Socially it means recreating a viable bourgeoisie, drawn from and participating in a wide variety of interests and activities, and regional centres capable of encouraging and sustaining these activities. Psychologically it means instilling a sense of worth into the population of the region by replacing the crippling colonialism of dependence with a feeling of equal participation in and contribution to the common national economy. These are most rigorous demands, the realization of which may require a generation or longer to accomplish. Nor are they difficult to accomplish simply because of the problems of developing a viable industry. Despite the historical experience out of which the present situation has developed, the problem is a new one of the 1970s and attempts at its solution must reflect the concerns of the present world. Limited resources, the dangers of unfettered industrial development, the pollution crisis, and other problems of the late twentieth century must necessarily shape much of the thinking of the architects of regional development. As well, of course, this thrust to development, occurring half a century later than that of most of eastern North America, is able to benefit both from the latter's experience and from the most recent industrial technology.

There are several lessons to be learned from this experience. Perhaps the most important is that industrialization is only one means of creating a reasonable living standard for a society. Rather than unrestricted growth, the region needs a modest industrial potential providing opportunities for both workers and entrepreneurs; the ideal of the "Pittsburgh of the North," even were its realization possible in the Maritimes, is part of the aspiration of another age. This is not to denigrate the role of secondary industry: one of the great strengths of a national policy is to provide the stability of protected domestic markets, a condition desperately needed by the narrowly specialized resource-based economy of the Maritimes. More important is the development of an integrated balanced economy in which secondary industry is strengthened, as are agriculture, mining, fish and woods industries, and financial and merchandising institutions. As a focus for these activities, strong regional urban centres are essential as a milieu in which to provide strong primary markets for regional output. Yet, while recognizing the significance of such centres, it is important that any development program maintain a balance among city, town, and rural communities. The city of Halifax, with half the population of the region, might have its attractions, but much that is distinctive and important in the Maritime way of life has been a product of the particular social organization of small scattered communities. Maritimers, like French Canadians before them, might well learn that one cannot separate form from substance. Unrestrained urbanization may produce the conditions which will destroy much of what it was designed to protect. Moreover, metropolises of whatever size cannot be separated from their hinterlands. The one great danger of the growth-centres concept is the assumption that three or four major urban centres can be developed in the region and that their natural hinterlands can be allowed to seek their own economic salvation.[38] The interaction of the metropolis with its hinterland is a subtle and reciprocal process and the economic well-being and social structures of the two elements are too intimately connected to admit to such precious rationalizations. As well, any development program must take care to maintain a balance between national or international corporations on the one hand and small regional concerns on the other. Both have major roles to play in regional development, and failure to protect the latter could have serious consequences. Finally, care must be taken to maintain a balance between private and public capital; it is essential that in all major endeavours the extensive public interest in most firms be protected by direct provincial involvement in the concern as a minority shareholder.

The task of development of the Maritime provinces will be no simple one as federal and provincial agencies have long since determined. The process will be one of slow and often costly experimentation. Yet, despite its costs and frustrations, the burden is a moral and social responsibility which the Canadian state cannot refuse. That state annexed the region in 1867 and partially integrated the regional economy in the late nineteenth century. Maritime eschatology since that time has not been predicated upon the destruction of the national policy but upon its fulfillment. And that fulfillment cannot be realized so long as a largely exploitative economic relationship exists between the region and its Central Canadian metropolis. Like the British before them, Central Canadians must accept the responsibility of empire and through the great instruments of state provide the support and protection upon which a stable, broad industrial structure can re-emerge in the Maritime region.

NOTES

1. For example, see the changing composition of the non-native-born population of Canada West between 1842 and 1871 found in the *Census of Canada* (1870-71), Vol. I, p. 136, and Vol. IV, pp. 136, 182, 258. The great majority of the non-native-born were immigrants from the United Kingdom. In 1842 about half the British emigrants were Irish, a majority of whom were probably of Protestant origin. Nine years later the Irish-born had more than doubled in number, most of the newcomers being Roman Catholic. After 1851 the Irish migrant was replaced by the English, and by 1871 the English-born rivalled the Irish-born in numbers. The impact of these shifts on the culture of the receiving country can be appreciated only when it is realized that the non-native born comprised between 25 and 42

per cent of the colony's population during this period, and that the majority of the native-born population were children of these immigrants.

2. The British had great impact on the population of New Brunswick, Prince Edward Island, Cape Breton, and the north shore of Nova Scotia, but were little found on the western peninsula of Nova Scotia. Unfortunately, gross census figures on birthplace are not available for New Brunswick and Nova Scotia before 1861, about a decade after the cessation of the major immigration to the Maritimes. These later figures may be found in the *Census of Canada* (1870-71), Vol. IV, pp. 174, 335, 346, 362.

3. The best discussion of this phenomenon is found in David S. Macmillan, "The 'New Man' in Action: Scottish Mercantile and Shipping Operations in the North American Colonies, 1760-1825," *Canadian Business History: Selected Studies, 1497-1971,* ed. D.S. Macmillan (Toronto, 1972), pp. 44-103.

4. Ibid.

5. Wilfred Harrison, "The Maritime Bank of the Dominion of Canada, 1872-1887" (M.A. Report, University of New Brunswick, 1970), chap. II.

6. See particularly the enumeration of newly formed American lumbering firms in southern New Brunswick found in the *New Brunswick Courier,* 8 August 1835 and 18 June 1836.

7. Harold Davis, *An International Community on the St. Croix* (Orono, Maine, 1950), chap. XVIII.

8. *New Brunswick Courier,* 2 February 1842. The Saint John Board of Trade balanced New Brunswick's trade in the following way:

Total value of imports	£ 1,257,300
Total earnings on exports	£ 1,278,445
Surplus	£ 21,145

Components of export earnings:	
Value of exports	£ 639,349
N.B. ships sold in Great Britain	£ 181,717
Freightage on N.B. produce to Great Britain	£ 247,629
Freightage on other produce to Great Britain	£ 87,500
Foreign vessels laden at Saint John	£ 86,250
English bills	£ 36,000
	£ 1,278,445

9. O.J. McDiarmid, *Commercial Policy in the Canadian Economy* (Cambridge, Mass., 1946), chap. VI.

10. Ibid., pp. 155-60.

11. *Canadian Manufacturer,* 7 September 1883; 2 November 1888.

12. H.G. J. Aitken, "Government and Business in Canada: An Interpretation," *Business History Review,* XXXVII-XXXVIII (1964), pp. 4-21.

13. T.W. Acheson, "The Social Origins of Canadian Industrialism: A Study in the Structure of Entrepreneurship, 1880-1910" (PH.D. thesis, University of Toronto, 1971), chap. III.
14. T.W. Acheson, "The Maritimes and the National Policy, 1880-1910," *Acadiensis,* I (2), pp. 4-12.
15. Generally speaking the 1891 census reveals that employers profited more from the woods industries and employees gained more from the new industries. For example, not only did workers in the foundry and sugar industries make twice the wages of sawmill workers, but the owners of the latter received a much smaller return on their investment. In 1890 sawmill operators had investments of $7.3 million (in land, buildings, machinery, and working capital) on which they earned $2.7 million (after paying costs of wages and raw materials); their earnings exceeded the total wages which they paid to 11,800 employees. By contrast, foundry and machine-works operators earned $0.5 million on an investment of $3.2 million, and sugar refinery owners made $0.2 million on an investment of $1.7 million. See: Canada, *Census 1890-91,* Vol. III, pp. 163-64; 119-21, 292-95; 323.
16. Acheson, "Maritimes and National Policy, 1880-1910," pp. 20-27.
17. *Annual Financial Review* (1923), pp. 111, 126.
18. Canada, *Sessional Papers,* XVIII (1885), Nos. 37, 37a, "Reports Relative to Manufacturing Industries in Existence in Canada."
19. There are no figures on personal income per capita before 1926. However, all evidence indicates that the greatest comparative decline in Maritime per-capita income occurred between 1919 and 1929. Evidence to support this contention for the period after 1925 is provided by R.O. Rowland in his study, *Some Regional Aspects of Canada's Economic Development,* prepared in 1957 for the Royal Commission on Canada's Economic Prospects. This study shows that personal incomes in the Maritimes were falling behind the national average in the years 1926-28, that they held relatively constant between 1929 and 1937, fell behind again in 1937-42, but narrowed the gap between 1943 and 1946 as a result of war expenditures. Between 1947 and 1951 the Maritime per-capita income declined steadily in comparison with the national average; after 1951 the gap between the two was once again narrowed but this was the result of federal government transfer payments which in the period 1951-55 averaged 11.6 per cent of personal income in the region (vs. 2.2 per cent in 1926). See Rowland, pp. 61-73; see also *Atlantic Provinces Statistical Review* (Atlantic Provinces Economic Council; hereafter A.P.E.C., 1974), p. 85.
20. *Historical Statistics of Canada,* ed. M.C. Urquhart and K.A.H. Buckley (Toronto, 1965), p. 22, series A221-232. Emigration between 1901 and 1931 was estimated by Keyfitz to have totalled 273,000 among Maritimers over the age of ten. Nearly half of this emigration occurred in the decade 1921 to 1931 and was so severe in Nova Scotia that the population over ten years of age actually declined during that time.
21. *Census of Canada* (1931), Vol. III, pp. 464, 468, 472, 476, 482, 486. Despite the supposed attractions of the Prairie West for the sons of Maritime farmers only 9,799 Maritimers were found in Saskatchewan and 7,482 in

Alberta. British Columbia was a more popular destination, claiming nearly
19,000 Maritime-born in 1931, a phenomenon which perhaps reflects the
fact that the timber economy of B.C. was more congenial to Maritime
workers than was the alien culture of wheat farming.
22. *Canada Year Book,* 1931, pp. 406-509; 1937, pp. 441-42. Manufactured
output in the Maritimes declined in value from $225,000,000 in 1917 to
$137,000,000 in 1921. After that it increased to $170,000,000 in 1929
(Canadian output on the same dates ranged from $2.8 billion to $2.9 billion
to $4.0 billion). Employment in Maritime industry fell from 49,000 in 1917
to 28,000 in 1921, then rose to an interwar high of 41,000 in 1929. By 1934
it had fallen to 29,000. (Canadian employment was 621,000, 456,000, and
693,000 on the first three dates.)
23. Canada, *Maritime Provinces in Their Relation to the National Economy of
Canada* (Ottawa, 1934), pp. 59-60.
24. Ibid., pp. 57-60, 64.
25. Rowland estimated in 1957 that the Atlantic provinces pulp and paper
output was consumed in equal portions by the British, the American, and
the regional markets. However most Newfoundland output was sold in the
United Kingdom while Maritime producers concentrated on the American
market, Rowland, *Some Regional Aspects of Canada's Economic
Development,* p. 22. In 1966 the Atlantic Provinces Economic Council
estimated that 63.5 per cent of all exports from the Atlantic provinces went
to the United States; presumably a much higher proportion of Maritime
exports would have done so, *Third Annual Review: The Atlantic Economy*
(A.P.E.C., 1969), pp. 37-39. For a brief historical survey of the development of
the New Brunswick pulp and paper industry to 1972 see the "Report of the
Industrial Inquiry Commission on the Pulp and Paper Industry in New
Brunswick" (Fredericton, 1972), chap. III. The initiative for pulp and paper
development in this province shifted from local leaders prior to the First
World War, to American leadership in the interwar period, to a
combination of local, American, European, and British Columbian
leadership after 1960.
26. E. R. Forbes, "The Maritime Rights Movement, 1919-1927: A Study in
Canadian Regionalism" (PH.D. thesis, Queen's University 1975), chap. IV.
27. This idea is suggested by B. S. Kierstead in *A Theory of Economic Change*
(Toronto, 1948), chap. XIII.
28. The decline is perhaps best illustrated in Halifax and Saint John. In 1880
there were 671 people in the former and 358 in the latter employed in the
needle trades; by 1931 the numbers had dropped to 49 and 230. By
comparison those in Montreal had risen from 6,000 in 1880 to 32,000 in
1930 and in Toronto from 2,000 to 20,000. In 1930 over one-third of all
manufacturing employment in Montreal and one-quarter of that in Toronto
was provided in the clothing industries; the comparable ratios for Halifax
and Saint John were 1 in 50 and 1 in 10. See Canada, *Census of 1881,* Vol.
III, pp. 354-59; 384-89, and *Census of 1931,* Vol. VIII, pp. 738-39.
29. See Canada, *Census of 1891,* Vol. III, pp. 178-83, 190-91; *Canada Year
Book,* 1952, pp. 689-90, 697.

30. In 1966 nearly 64 per cent of all Atlantic provinces exports went to the United States, and the proportion of Maritime provinces exports to the United States would have been considerably higher. The international economy was more important to the Atlantic provinces than it was to the nation as a whole (exports accounted for nearly 20 per cent of the gross regional product as opposed to only 16 per cent of the gross national product). Products of the forests, mines, and fisheries accounted for 85 per cent of regional exports. Third Annual Review, *The Atlantic Economy* (A.P.E.C., 1969), pp. 36-40.

31. Roy E. George, *A Leader and a Laggard: Manufacturing Industry in Nova Scotia, Quebec, and Ontario* (Toronto, 1970), chaps. 3-9.

32. Ibid., p. 13.

33. C. R. Marks estimated that this figure had been reached as early as 1964. See "Defence Services in the Atlantic Provinces" (A.P.E.C., 1965), pp. 12-13.

34. Statistics Canada reported in 1971 that there were 11,700 people engaged in Maritime provincial administration; 14,790 in the non-military federal administration (another 32,360 were in military service); and 5,180 in local administration. There were 31,620 engaged in the public administration of the three provinces and, as this total does not include civil servants such as provincial social workers, the figure is actually much higher (in New Brunswick for example, the census lists 5,755 persons in provincial administration; the New Brunswick civil service in 1971 comprised 6,759 persons). There were thus far more employees in the public administration than in the combined forestry (9,935), woods industries (8,010), and pulp and paper industries (10,615); and more than in the combined fishing (9,955) and fish processing (14,845) industries. There were nearly twice as many workers in the public administration as in the whole agricultural sector (19,620). The growth of the public service is perhaps best illustrated in New Brunswick where the numbers of civil servants rose from 2,080 in 1951 to 2,767 in 1960-61, to 6,759 in 1971. See Canada, *1971 Census*, Cat. 94-740, Industries, pp. 2/11-2/12; New Brunswick Civil Service Commission *Annual Report* (1961), p. 28; ibid., (1973), p. 9.

35. Canada, *1971 Census*, Cat. 94-741, Table 3A; Canada, *1961 Census*, Cat. 94-551, Table 12. Between 1951 and 1971 the proportion of the Canadian work force employed in primary and secondary industry fell from 45 per cent to 28 per cent; the comparable proportions in the Maritime provinces were 43 per cent and 23 per cent.

36. Typical of the Maritime experience was the growth of the New Brunswick provincial revenues. In 1946 these totalled $18.7 million, largely derived from liquor and gasoline taxes (federal subsidies amounted to less than one-sixth of the total). The Dominion-Provincial Tax Agreement of 1947 nearly tripled the federal contribution to the provincial treasury and raised provincial revenues to $27 million in 1948. For the next decade revenues showed a slow but steady growth reaching $57 million in 1957. That year the federal government initiated its program of equalization grants and the federal contribution rose to nearly half of provincial revenues. Between 1959 and 1974 federal subsidies rose from $31 million to $158 million,

provincial income taxes from nothing to $95 million, and total provincial revenues from $69 to $485 million. Even these figures greatly underestimate the federal contribution to the province since they do not include shared-cost agreements. In 1974, for example, the federal government contributed $71.6 million to health and $28.8 million to welfare services in New Brunswick. The diversity and complexity of provincial government operations and services parallelled this rising income. In particular, the government involvement in industrial development strategies through the medium of the New Brunswick Electric Power Commission, the New Brunswick Industrial Finance Board, the New Brunswick Research and Productivity Council, the New Brunswick Development Corporation, and the provincial Department of Economic Growth, began in the mid-1950s and reached a peak in the early 1970s. By 1974 the province had guaranteed or made loans totalling $47 million to industries, agencies, and enterprises. In addition, the Department of Regional Economic Growth was committing several millions of dollars annually to the provision of industrial services through industrial parks and industrial research. See *Public Accounts of New Brunswick,* 1940-1974.

37. J. P. Francis and N. G. Pillai, "Regional Development and Regional Policy—Some Issues and Recent Canadian Experience" (D.R.E.E., 1973), pp. 52-62.
38. The idea has been discussed in the Sixth Annual Review of *The Atlantic Economy* (Atlantic Provinces Economic Council, 1972), pp. 57-62.

T. D. REGEHR

Western Canada and the Burden of National Transportation Policies

Transportation and transportation costs are of vital concern in a country as large as Canada. They are of particular importance to the more isolated areas such as the western interior of the continent. These areas generally pay more for transportation, simply because of the distances involved. In western Canada, however, transportation costs are further increased by a discriminatory rate structure which has been built into all Canadian transcontinental transportation policies.

No single issue has contributed more to western Canadian discontent within Confederation than the so-called national transportation policies. Since 1883, when the first freight-rate schedule of the Canadian Pacific Railway was published, there has been deliberate and admitted freight-rate discrimination against the West. This discrimination was ameliorated, but not removed, when western governments and politicians resorted to unilateral action in defiance of national policies and secured freight rate reductions. Such unilateral action was loudly denounced as very dangerous to Confederation, to national unity, and to national policies. In fact it simply proved that the less populous and therefore politically less powerful regions cannot look to national policies to meet their requirements unless, in times of particular stress, they have the power, the means, and the will, to assert their demands and thus forcibly restructure unacceptable aspects of national policies.

"Fair Discrimination" Against the West

At the Western Economic Opportunities Conference held in Calgary, in July 1973, the background paper prepared by the federal government expressed sympathy for western problems and offered a few minor and short-term concessions. The writers of the federal background paper insisted, however, that nothing must be done to shift any portion of the western freight rate burden to other parts of the country. The federal writers argued that "the railways have to achieve a balance between their costs and revenues, taking into account the total spread of their operations and differing degrees of competition."[1]

The logic of the federal statement seems unassailable; yet it presents the core of the western transportation and freight-rate problem. The difficulty arises because of differing degrees of competition in the various regions of Canada. In one region the railways must meet very vigorous competition, both from rival American railroads and from water transport on the Great Lakes and St. Lawrence River system. In another region the railways have a virtual monopoly. National policies specifically permit and, indeed, require the railways to charge whatever the traffic of a particular region can be made to pay, subject only to fixed maximums set by the Board of Transportation Commissioners which are much higher in non-competitive than in competitive areas.[2] The railways set low rates, or reduce their rates, wherever competition from other railways or from other forms of transport compel them to do so, even if those reduced rates lead to operations losses in the affected region. In areas where no effective competition exists the railways set their rates at much higher levels. If the railways are forced to operate uneconomical sections, or if there are operational losses in highly competitive areas, they recoup those losses by charging higher rates in non-competitive areas. The federal regulatory agencies have repeatedly described the resulting rate differentials between the competitive St. Lawrence region and the non-competitive prairie region as discriminatory, but the agencies have also consistently ruled that these differentials constitute "fair discrimination."[3]

The policy of "fair discrimination" is rooted in the National Policy first enunciated in 1878 and, more specifically, in the

1881 contract signed by the Canadian Pacific Railway syndicate on the one hand, and the federal government on the other. Both parties to that agreement were well aware of the magnitude of the task in hand. Building a transcontinental railway along an all-Canadian route was very difficult and very expensive. Massive government subsidies were provided to assist in the construction. Once built, however, the new railway faced additional and very serious operational problems. Fully one-half of the new line passed through areas where little or no local traffic could be expected. There would certainly be operational deficits on such mileage, the longest "unproductive" stretches being north of Lake Superior and through the British Columbia interior.

Much of the remaining mileage served the St. Lawrence region where very stiff competition from rival railways and from water transport was certain. Water transport in particular posed problems, since most of the canals and harbour facilities throughout the St. Lawrence and Great Lakes shipping system had been built as public undertakings and were made available to shippers free of charge or upon payment of only nominal tolls. The railways had to maintain their own rights of way and station facilities, while holding at least their summer rates at the low competitive levels set by water carriers. It was therefore very unlikely that the Canadian Pacific Railway would earn sufficient operational surpluses in Ontario and Quebec to offset the anticipated deficits north of Lake Superior and in British Columbia.

The prairie region was still largely unsettled and was not expected to generate large volumes of traffic for many years. It nevertheless offered the Canadian Pacific Railway the prospect of sufficient surpluses to permit a balancing of its national accounts. Water transport at reasonable cost was not a factor on the prairies and, from the beginning, the syndicate insisted that all American railway competition be kept out of the region.[4] Without any competition to contend with, the syndicate intended to set its western rates at a sufficiently high level to offset the anticipated losses north of Lake Superior. George Stephen, the first president of the Canadian Pacific Railway, was convinced that his company would not be viable unless it held a western monopoly which would force all traffic to and from the prairies onto its lines at high rates. Without a monopoly west of Winnipeg he believed "the whole line from Winnipeg to Ottawa would be rendered all but useless, and the large sums of money spent, and to be spent thereon, might as well have been thrown in the lake."[5] He believed that "no sane man would give one dollar for the whole line east of Winnipeg," if the West enjoyed the same competitive conditions as prevailed in the East. The loss of prairie traffic to American roads, or western rate reductions sufficient to hold that traffic by competitive means, would, in George Stephen's opinion, "in a very short time make it impossible to operate the C.P.R. east of Winnipeg."[6]

The only alternative to discriminatory western rates in 1881 was a federal operating subsidy for the Lake Superior and British Columbia sections. Both of Canada's major political parties, however, were fiercely determined that no public funds be used to subsidize C.P.R. operations.[7] Both considered construction subsidies entirely proper, but never seriously considered lightening the western rate burden by offering the company operational subsidies. The western monopoly and the freight-rate discrimination it facilitated were therefore approved, and the basis of a troublesome national transportation policy was laid. Rates on traffic east of Thunder Bay were set to meet American railway and heavily subsidized Great Lakes and St. Lawrence water transport competition. Rates west of Thunder Bay, on the other hand, were protected by monopoly and set in a manner which would allow the railway to balance its total costs and revenues. Competition was the criterion in the East, while the railway's total needs were the determining factor in monopoly-protected western rate-making.[8]

The results were predictable. The first western rate schedule published by the C.P.R. appeared in 1883. It set a rate for wheat which was almost three times that for comparable distances in competitive eastern areas. The rate was 21.6 cents per bushel from Winnipeg to Thunder Bay. Wheat shipped from Moose Jaw to Thunder Bay was carried at 30.6 cents per bushel.[9] The rate from Thunder Bay to the seaboard, covering a distance about twice that from Winnipeg to Thunder Bay but subject to water competition, was 15 cents per bushel. The summer rate for grain on the Grand Trunk Railway and later on the C.P.R. between Toronto and Montreal, a distance nearly as great as that from Winnipeg to Thunder Bay, was well below 10 cents per bushel.

The price of wheat at Thunder Bay in the 1880s was approximately 65 cents per bushel. The freight rates therefore threatened to consume half of the farmer's gross income from his grain crop and placed an intolerable burden on the struggling pioneer homesteaders. When, as was the case in 1883, the wheat crop suffered serious frost damage, there was little, if anything, left after the farmer paid the freight charges and his immediate operating costs.[10]

The C.P.R. certainly did not earn exorbitant profits in the early years. High operating costs and sparse traffic on the long mileage north of Lake Superior, and difficult operating conditions in the Rockies, took care of any surpluses generated by traffic going to or coming from the prairies.[11] The defenders of the National Policy did not think this an unfair arrangement. After all, the entire line from Ottawa west had been built to open up and develop the West. There was therefore no reason why western traffic should not meet the operating costs of the entire line. This argument failed to acknowledge that, as far as the West was concerned, a cheap and direct line running south of Lake Superior might have carried their products to export markets at much lower rates. The "national" Lake Superior section was not built merely as a service to the West. It was accepted as the instrument which would tie the western traffic to the Canadian metropolitan centres in the St. Lawrence lowlands. Far from being simply a generous and magnanimous gesture to the West, the Lake Superior line was also an instrument of Canadian nationalism and eastern Canadian economic imperialism.[12] It was built because of fears that western traffic shipped along a railway south of Lake Superior would not find its way to Toronto and Montreal, but would pass instead through New York on its way to world markets. Westerners have never understood why they and they alone should be charged with the operating deficits on that "national" mileage.

Canadian railway officials and the federal regulatory agencies sometimes allude to the fact that American transportation policies also permit discriminatory rates against non-competitive regions.[13] Farmers in the American Midwest, of course, find it as difficult as their Canadian counterparts to understand and accept the concept of "fair discrimination," and they have successfully demanded huge government grants and subsidies to build a highway system on which trucks can offer effective competition, thus bringing their western rates down. The substantially greater transcontinental distances in Canada make that solution less practical and certainly much more expensive.

Sometimes the railways and federal agencies also maintain that operating costs on the Canadian prairies are higher than in eastern Canada.[14] A harsher climate, the seasonal nature of much of the agricultural traffic, and the fact that the bulky grain trade is all one way (thus necessitating extensive deadheading of empty grain cars), all add to western operating costs. Higher rates in the West, it is alleged, are therefore justified, although some very similar operating disadvantages for many eastern commodities are seldom mentioned.

It is important to point out that the railways do not calculate, or at least refuse to reveal, regional operating costs. Such costs, in any case, have never been the basis for regional rate-making. Western Canadians have long, but entirely unsuccessfully, demanded effective regional cost accounting and cost disclosures by the railways, and the implementation of regional rates commensurate with regional costs. The railways and the federal agencies have never agreed to do this. They believe "fair discrimination" is absolutely essential if they are to "balance their costs and revenues, taking into account the total spread of their operations and differing degrees of competition."[15]

The national policy of permitting "fair discrimination" against non-competitive regions created enormous economic, political, and constitutional problems in Western Canada. In the 1880s Premier John Norquay of Manitoba and many of his supporters believed the problem of high freight rates would be resolved if and when the prairie region was opened up to American railroad competition. Norquay was not particularly concerned about the problems of the C.P.R. elsewhere, and he chartered local railway companies which were expected to make connections at the international boundary with American railroads.

The province of Manitoba apparently had the power to charter local railway lines, including those running to the border, but the federal government decided to disallow such provincial charters on grounds that they were not in the interests of the Dominion. This disallowance policy, exercised repeatedly as Manitoba continued to pass railway charters which Ottawa found objectionable, transformed the economic problem into a political and constitutional dispute. The interests and policies of one region of the country had come into sharp conflict with a basic aspect of national policy, and Sir Charles Tupper, the federal minister of railways, summed up the situation when he said in the House of Commons, "Are the interests of Manitoba and the North-west to be sacrificed to the policy of Canada? I say, if it is necessary — yes."[16]

An effective federal system should provide the means whereby a province or region whose interests are blatantly flouted can have effective political and constitutional recourse. In the years after 1883 Premier Norquay tried all the political and constitutional procedures available to him in his efforts to resolve the railway problem. He travelled repeatedly to Ottawa to explain the problem, to present petitions, and to seek assistance. He certainly was willing to consider compromises, provided Manitoba's basic transportation needs were met. In Ottawa he did receive a number of minor concessions, but Sir John A. Macdonald was determined that the basic provisions of his railway policy remain unchanged. Letters, petitions, and warnings from western members of Parliament, from western boards of trade, from the press, and from local party officials and workers all failed to move the prime minister. When warned that violence and an agitation for Manitoba's secession from Confederation were imminent, he attributed the difficulty to discontented Liberals and broken land speculators,[17] and inquired of the Colonial Office if imperial troops would be available if the national policies led to armed confrontations between federal authorities and western farmers.[18]

By 1887 the magnitude of the problem had become clear. A national policy entirely unacceptable to one region of the country had been implemented, and all proper political and constitutional devices open to the aggrieved region had been exhausted. W.B. Scarth, a Conservative member of Parliament representing a Manitoba constituency, clearly recognized the problem. He wrote to the prime minister: "I remember my dear Sir John that when I was a resident of Ontario you used sometimes to say when Manitoba was kicking that it only had five votes. Five votes are not many now, but if your majority were only fifteen instead of what it is five votes would count."[19] The five Manitoba votes, of course, counted for very much less with Macdonald than did the ninety-two from Ontario and the sixty-five from Quebec, and most of the Ontario and Quebec members were pleased with the national transportation policy. The federal Liberals, despite considerable huffing and puffing against the C.P.R. monopoly, were as adamant as the Conservatives in opposing government operating subsidies or eastern rate increases. Yet, in order to remain viable in the early years, the Canadian Pacific either had to retain its high western rates or had to obtain government subsidies to operate the Lake Superior and British Columbia sections. Both national parties were in basic agreement regarding the choice between those two alternatives.

Macdonald was so sure of eastern support for his transportation policy that he even authorized Scarth to promise his constituents in the 1887 election that he, Scarth, would introduce in the House of Commons a motion of want of confidence in his own party's transportation policy. Scarth thought this was the only way to save his Conservative seat in Manitoba.[20] The transportation policy certainly would not have been endangered, even if Scarth had actually introduced his promised motion. Within the Canadian federal structure a region with only 5 votes out of 242 had virtually no chance of altering fixed national policies, no matter how determined the region's representative might be.

Manitoba's Unilateral Action to Remove "Fair Discrimination"
The railway problems of Western Canada were not ameliorated until the provincial government of Manitoba resorted to unilateral action, the threat of violence, and open defiance of the

federal government and its policies. Norquay's moderate policies of negotiations, conferences, petitions, and accommodation led only to his removal from office. In 1888 he was replaced by Thomas Greenway, a Liberal who promised to build a railway from Winnipeg to Emerson and bring in American competition, even if such a policy led to armed confrontations between federal and provincial authorities. After a final and seemingly fruitless visit to Ottawa, Greenway went to Chicago and St. Paul to enlist American financial and political support for his program.[21] There were even rumours that the premier was also looking for American military support.

Greenway's show of determination accomplished within a matter of weeks what all the politics of federalism during the previous seven years had failed to accomplish. The federal government abandoned its policy of disallowance, bought out the C.P.R. monopoly, and granted that company sufficient financial assistance to allow it to withstand American competition.[22] The provincial railway to Emerson was immediately built and a running rights agreement with the Northern Pacific Railroad negotiated.

One of the conditions under which the American Company entered Canada on the provincially built railway was that it would set its initial rates at 85 per cent of the then prevailing C.P.R. rates. The C.P.R. immediately responded with a 15-per-cent rate reduction of its own. Competition had arrived in Western Canada. Premier Greenway and his cohorts were convinced that the initial 15-per-cent reduction would mark only the beginning of a competitive battle between the C.P.R. and the Northern Pacific Railroad which would drive western rates down to the levels prevalent in the East. In this the Manitobans were sorely disappointed. The truth of the matter was that the American railways, like their Canadian counterparts, were far more interested in maximizing profits than in competing with one another just for the sake of competition. Both roads operated under rate structures which were higher in the West where the railways enjoyed a natural monopoly than in the East where they had to face competition from water transport. Neither was eager to see drastic reductions in western rates, and the C.P.R. and the Northern Pacific soon reached an informal agreement under which the Northern Pacific agreed to refrain from competitive raids and rate-cutting in Manitoba. In return the C.P.R. promised to discontinue its attempt to attract American traffic at Puget Sound to its lines. For the Northern Pacific the new Manitoba connection was simply a device to force the C.P.R. to "play fair" in Washington.[23] No really effective competition developed in Manitoba.

The crucial factor leading to lower rates in Central and Eastern Canada was competition from water transport, not competition from rival American roads. Lack of similar competition in Western Canada blunted and nearly nullified Manitoba's first assault on the national transportation policies. Further significant western rate reductions were only achieved in 1897 and 1901 when once again westerners threatened open defiance of national policies in their determination to create a competitive transportation system in the West. Only then was the burden of national transportation policies significantly reduced and the ratio between eastern and western rates substantially altered.

In 1897 the Canadian Pacific Railway, which had always been determined to keep Western Canada as its economic preserve, found itself vulnerable when rich mineral deposits were discovered in the Kootenay District of southeastern British Columbia. The C.P.R. mainline through Rogers' Pass was too far away to serve this region adequately, and American railways began to move in. Officials of the C.P.R. sought federal assistance to build their own line from Lethbridge, Alberta, to Nelson, British Columbia, via the Crow's Nest Pass. The federal government knew that such assistance would be opposed by many eastern politicians who could foresee no immediate benefit for their region. It would also be very unpopular in Western Canada unless some major concessions were offered on the most serious western transportation grievances. Federal assistance for a new C.P.R. line would obviously enhance the practical monopoly that company still enjoyed in Western Canada.[24] There were, moreover, other railway contractors and promoters eager and willing to take on the Crow's Nest Pass project. Foremost among these were William Mackenzie and Donald Mann, both former C.P.R. contractors who, in 1896, became promoters of a new western Canadian and later transcontinental Canadian Northern Railway system. They were very eager to secure the federal contract to build the Crow's Nest Pass Railway in 1897.

It is not clear what concessions Mackenzie and Mann offered in 1897. They did negotiate with the federal government and with the provincial governments of British Columbia and Manitoba, offering to build across southern British Columbia all the way to Vancouver if offered sufficient aid. They presented their railway as the only one which might eventually compete effectively with the c.p.r. American competition had failed, but a new hope was rising.

Premier Turner of British Columbia found the Mackenzie and Mann proposals sufficiently attractive to vote them substantial subsidies. These, however, were not sufficient to get the railway across southern British Columbia built and connected with the Manitoba mileage controlled by Mackenzie and Mann. The two promoters had to go to Ottawa to seek federal aid for their project. The promise of independent action in British Columbia certainly complicated the negotiations in Ottawa. The federal government was inclined to deal with the c.p.r., but for a time President Van Horne and Vice-President Shaughnessy were not willing to match the concessions offered by Mackenzie and Mann. At one point the c.p.r. men were prepared to see the entire Crow's Nest Pass contract go to Mackenzie and Mann.[25]

Mackenzie and Mann, despite their ambitious and visionary proposals, were weak contenders in 1897. They controlled many railway charters, but only 125 miles of track in actual operation, and that was 800 miles from the proposed Crow's Nest Pass line. They depended on the c.p.r. and the Northern Pacific Railroad for all rail connections to points outside Manitoba, and any rate concessions they could make in 1897 depended on the kind of rate divisions they could get from the transcontinentals on through traffic. The federal government therefore continued its negotiations with the c.p.r.[26]

The offer made by Mackenzie and Mann in 1897 did not get them the Crow's Nest Pass contract, but it significantly increased the likelihood of provincial action in opposition to the federal program unless the federal plan included significant rate reductions. The c.p.r. was very reluctant to make such reductions, but in the end President Van Horne decided his company should make sufficient concessions to obtain the Crow's Nest

Pass contract. The mere presence of potential competitors in 1897 paid handsome dividends for western shippers.

The terms of the Crow's Nest Pass contract provided a federal subsidy of $11,000 per mile for the proposed 330-mile line. This was expected to cover approximately two-thirds of the estimated construction costs. In return for this subsidy the C.P.R. agreed to reduce its western freight rates on a wide range of products by approximately 20 per cent. The crucial rate on grain was reduced from 17 cents to 14 cents per hundredweight from Winnipeg to Thunder Bay. These reductions were only obtained because western politicians were determined to resist and oppose any federal subsidies for the C.P.R. unless these were coupled with rate reductions, and because rival promoters were available and made plausible the threat of independent provincial action.

The Crow's Nest Pass rates did not bring western rates down to the same levels as prevailed in Central Canada, and many western farmers and the provincial government of Manitoba continued to demand further reductions. Increases in the volume of western traffic carried by the C.P.R. made it possible for the company to absorb the 1897 rate reductions without serious difficulty, but neither the C.P.R. nor the federal government thought any further reductions could be justified. A new threat, or perhaps the reality of railway competition, was needed before rates would be further reduced.

In 1901 Mackenzie and Mann offered Manitobans an opportunity to provide the necessary competitive pressure which would result in further reductions of western freight rates. Their failure to obtain the Crow's Nest Pass contract had slowed and altered but not halted the railway schemes of Mackenzie and Mann. By 1901 they were busily at work extending their small Manitoba system eastward to Port Arthur and westward towards Prince Albert and Edmonton. Operationally their railway differed markedly from the C.P.R. The Canadian Northern at that time was simply a prairie system, and Mackenzie and Mann were quite willing to set their rates, according to operating and capital costs actually incurred. They did not have to take into account any operating deficits north of Lake Superior, although they could send all the traffic originating on or destined for their prairie lines east over the lines of the established railroads at rates determined by Great Lakes water transport. Mackenzie and Mann could afford to make further rate reductions and still operate at a profit. In 1901 they agreed to do so in return for substantial government assistance.[27]

The construction of the line from Winnipeg to Port Arthur was well advanced in 1901, but it created serious financing problems for Mackenzie and Mann. At the same time, the Northern Pacific Railroad, which had been brought into Manitoba with such enthusiasm in 1888, indicated that it intended to sell its Manitoba lines, preferably to the C.P.R. There was consequently great fear that the C.P.R. might take over both the tired Northern Pacific and the financially embarrassed Canadian Northern Railway, thus re-establishing a complete monopoly in Western Canada.

Mackenzie and Mann were convinced that their system could and would become a very effective competitor of the C.P.R., if it could obtain the funds to complete the line to Port Arthur, and if it could acquire the Northern Pacific mileage. Premier Roblin of Manitoba did not like the prospect of a re-established C.P.R. monopoly and was willing to help the Canadian Northern. He insisted, however, that the anticipated competitive benefits promised by Mackenzie and Mann be written into the agreement he would sign with them. The result was an agreement whereby the Manitoba government guaranteed Canadian Northern construction bonds for the entire mileage from Winnipeg to Port Arthur. The Manitoba government also leased the Northern Pacific lines and then reassigned the lease to the Canadian Northern. In return, the Canadian Northern agreed to further substantial western freight-rate reductions. The rate for grain, which was considered of the greatest importance, was to be cut from 14 cents to 10 cents per hundredweight, Winnipeg to Port Arthur.[28]

On the strength of the assistance thus granted, the Canadian Northern Railway became a regional railway of Western Canada which set its freight rates as only a regional railway could. The C.P.R., of course, had to lower its western rates to remain competitive. At first only rates at C.P.R. points which also had Canadian Northern connections were reduced, but eventually the reductions were applied across Manitoba. Similar but somewhat smaller reductions were granted on traffic in the Northwest Territories. Only increased traffic volumes and a very cautious developmental policy enabled the C.P.R. to continue effective competition with its new regional rival, which quickly built numerous developmental prairie lines that were initially not very profitable.

The action of the Manitoba government in dealing directly with a regional railway and unilaterally reducing regional rates without regard to national considerations was severely criticized by a number of Ontario and Quebec politicians. There was great concern that the stability of the national transportation policies would be upset. The federal politicians feared that Manitoba was disregarding the interests of other regions in the attempt to obtain lower prairie freight rates. Henri Bourassa expressed the apprehensions of many when he complained that the 1901 agreement "put in the hands of a provincial government a power that may be used at any time against the general interests of Canada."[29] Who would pay the operational deficits on the Lake Superior section if the Manitoba government, working in cooperation with a regional railway system, created a genuinely competitive rail system on the prairies?

No federal government was willing to initiate the kind of railway policies pursued by the Manitoba government in 1901. Yet, thanks to the determined action of the provincial government, western rates were significantly reduced and a new balance established between central, and western rates. It seems clear that the relief from the burdens imposed on Western Canada by the national transportation policies would not have come in 1901 without the unilateral action taken by Manitoba.

Premier Roblin was convinced that effective railway competition had become a reality in 1901. In his capacity as railways commissioner he proudly announced that his government had resolved, for all time to come, Manitoba's railway freight-rates problem. Unfortunately Roblin was quite mistaken. The western freight rates had certainly been reduced. Manitoba had established regional railway competition, but that competition proved of short duration, and western rates were substantially increased again.

Less than two years after Manitoba signed its agreement with the Canadian Northern Railway, the federal government introduced railway policies which eventually destroyed the advantages gained by Manitoba. In 1903 the federal government introduced legislation which provided enormous subsidies for the construction of a new transcontinental system – the National Transcontinental–Grand Trunk Pacific railways which were to link up with the eastern Grand Trunk Railway. This action by the federal government threatened to cut off many of the Canadian Northern Railway's connections in the East with the Grand Trunk. Consequently the Canadian Northern managers felt that under the circumstances they had no alternative but to expand their regional railway into a transcontinental system. They sought federal aid and by 1911 two new lines were being built across the bush and rock of the Canadian shield north of Lake Superior. The long-term operational prospects of the two new lines north of Lake Superior were certainly no better than those of the c.p.r. had been in 1881. With the construction of their own line north of Lake Superior, Mackenzie and Mann expanded their profitable regional railway into an unprofitable transcontinental service. The rates charged by the Canadian Northern in Western Canada were soon affected.

The financing of the new transcontinental mileage, coupled with wartime inflation and financial stringencies, ruined both the Canadian Northern Railway and the National Transcontinental – Grand Trunk Pacific systems.[30] The two still incomplete transcontinentals were taken over by the federal government, and in 1918 the federal Board of Railway Commissioners authorized the railways to raise their western rates above the levels set in the 1901 Manitoba agreement. The federal board ruled that that agreement, although in force for many years, was beyond the constitutional power of a province to enact. The board believed the regulation of all interprovincial traffic was a federal responsibility.[31] This ruling was immediately appealed, but ultimately upheld in the courts, and the rates set by the 1901 agreement were a thing of the past, although the more favourable ratio between central and western rates established by the 1901 agreement was maintained since both central and western rates rose by approximately the same percentage. In Western Canada rate increases up to the levels set by the Crow's Nest Pass Agreement were authorized. The Board of Railway Commissioners held that it did not have power to authorize increases beyond that level since the Crow's Nest Pass Agreement was incorporated in federal rather than provincial legislation.

Two years later inflation, and particularly a labour agitation for wage parity between Canadian and American railway workers, induced the federal government to authorize further rate increases. This time, under authority of the War Measures Act, the provisions of the Crow's Nest Pass Agreement were set aside, although again central and western rates were raised by approximately the same percentage.

The setting aside of the Manitoba agreement and the Crow's Nest Pass rates created very much dissatisfaction in Western Canada. It was one of the most important factors in the political success of the Progressive party in the federal election of 1921. The restoration of the Crow's Next Pass rates and significant tariff reductions were the two issues on which the frequently divided Progressives all agreed. The government that had set aside the Manitoba and Crow's Nest Pass rates was very decisively defeated in 1921, and Canada's first minority government was elected to office.

In this situation, and with the conciliatory William Lyon Mackenzie King as prime minister, the Progressives were able to obtain a partial restoration of the old rates. After some irritating delays, the Crow's Nest Pass rates for unprocessed cereal grains were restored, and they have remained in effect ever since. This restoration of the Crow's Nest Pass rates for cereal grains met the most important demands of western export-oriented agricultural producers. They wanted low rates to send their staple commodities to world markets, and the compromise of a partial restoration of the Crow's Nest Pass rates was accepted, if not cheered, in Western Canada.[32]

In 1923, after forty years of agitation and determined initiatives by the province of Manitoba, the freight-rate problems of western grain farmers had been significantly improved, but they had not been solved. The ratio between central and western rates had been altered in 1888, 1897, and 1901, and the altered ratios, if not the absolute rates, have remained fairly constant since 1923. Further, on those commodities of greatest importance to western grain farmers, the maximum rates set under the Crow's Nest Pass Agreement were re-established in 1923 and have not been altered since then. Both the altered ratios and the fixed rates on unprocessed grains are at least in part attributable to the direct action taken by the Manitoba government.

Industrialization and New Transportation Policies

Western Canada and the economic aspirations of Western Canadians have changed significantly since 1923. The freight-rate arrangements which were tolerated in 1923 are no longer acceptable. Three main reasons can be given for the renewed demands in Western Canada for an end to freight rates which discriminate against Western Canada on everything except unprocessed grain products. The first of these reasons is the effect of the so-called horizontal rate increases of the last thirty years; the second is the diversification and increased industrialization of the Western Canadian economy; and the third is the technological obsolescence of much of Western Canada's transportation and grain-handling system.

Since 1923 costs and prices of all goods and services have increased very substantially, particularly after 1945. The normal response to increased railway costs has been an application for rate increases. All the major rate increases since 1945, subject only to some comparatively minor and technical exceptions and to the provisions of the Crow's Nest Pass Agreement, have respected the ratio between central and western rates established by the Manitoba government in 1901. The railways have been authorized to increase their rates from time to time, but always by fixed percentages which were applied more or less equally to eastern, central, and western rates. Such fixed percentage increases, across the board, are referred to as horizontal increases.

Horizontal increases may sound fair, but they have been frequently denounced in Western Canada. They maintain and often exacerbate the discrimination built into the national rate structures. The western problem is best illustrated by a simple example. Let us assume a 30-per-cent increase is applied against a commodity rate which stood at 10 cents per hundredweight in Central Canada and at 20 cents per hundredweight in the West. Applying a 30-per-cent increase to both will make the new rates 13 and 26 cents per hundredweight respectively. The percentage increase is the same, but the net difference between the rates has increased from 10 to 13 cents. Firms and industries which were competitive in the less-favoured region when their rate was only 10 cents per hundredweight higher than that of their central rivals, might be unable to compete when that difference rises to 13 cents per hundredweight. As a result, each horizontal rate increase makes it more difficult for western businesses to compete with their more central counterparts.[33]

The Crow's Nest Pass rates have been consistently exempted from successive horizontal rate increases and have in fact become the best transportation bargain on the continent. It is this fact which makes the rate structure tolerable to many western grain farmers. Western Canada, however, is no longer the exclusive domain of the grain farmer. As technology and mechanization reduce the numbers of people needed to tend to the grain fields, there are more and more demands that western raw materials be processed in Western Canada, and that more new primary and secondary industries locate in the region. Unfortunately the discriminatory rate structure is a major obstacle to such economic diversification.

It is almost impossible for many western businesses and industries to compete with eastern rivals if the freight rates for everything they bring into the region and everything they send out are significantly higher than the comparable rates paid by their competitors. A few examples, shown in Table 1, illustrate the degree of discrimination between competitive and non-competitive regions still prevalent in our national railway rates structures, and clearly indicate the magnitude of the problem. In the examples given, Vancouver is considered a "competitive" point because of water transport available there. The prairie centers are not considered "competitive" points.[34]

Officially the Vancouver rates are justified as so-called long-haul rates, while the prairie rates are classed as short-haul rates.

Table 1 Examples of Freight Rates

From	To	Commodity	Rate/cwt.
Toronto	Vancouver	Canned goods	212
Morden	Vancouver	Canned goods	190
Toronto	Vancouver	Iron and steel products	168
Toronto	Saskatoon	Iron and steel products	247
Hamilton	Vancouver	Skelp	135
Hamilton	Edmonton	Skelp	211
Hamilton	Calgary	Structural steel	246
Hamilton	Vancouver	Structural steel	164

It has been demonstrated repeatedly, however, that the so-called long-haul rates have little or nothing to do with the distance the goods are hauled, and a good deal to do with the degree and extent of transportation competition at particular points. Vancouver long-haul rates, for example, were very significantly reduced when the Panama Canal was opened, thus making cities on the Pacific Coast truly competitive. The basic concept underlying all rate-making in Canada is competition, or the lack of it. Such rate-making is a very serious obstacle to any economic diversification or industrialization in regions which lack effective transportation competition and therefore suffer from high and discriminatory freight rates.

Even the discrimination inherent in the Crow's Nest Pass rates and generally considered very favourable to the West has become an obstacle to western economic diversification and development. The Crow's Nest rates apply only to unprocessed grain, while the "fair discrimination" rates are applied to processed or milled products. Thus grain is carried from Saskatoon to Moncton at 92 cents per hundredweight, but millfeed at 162 cents.[35] It was this rate structure which made it cheaper for the Quaker Oats Company to close down its large rolling mills and elevators in Saskatoon, next door to the fields where the oats are grown, and to expand and modernize their mills in Peterborough, Ontario.[36] The attempts to obtain a crushing plant to process the rapeseed grown in Saskatchewan have encountered similar problems. The fixed Crow's Nest Pass rates are too low, at least when compared with the high rates on processed grain products, to allow the establishment of extensive agricultural processing plants in Western Canada. Yet many prairie grain farmers are determined to resist any tampering with the Crow's Nest Pass rates, and a rural-urban, agricultural-industrial cleavage on this issue seems inevitable.

A third western transportation problem concerns the technological obsolescence of much of Western Canada's rail transportation and grain-handling systems. These systems were built in the late nineteenth and early twentieth centuries and have remained basically unchanged since that time. It is important to remember that the system was built at a time when few roads or highways were available. Consequently it was widely believed that every farmer must be within ten, or at most twenty, miles of a rural grain delivery point. The time and cost involved in hauling grain by sleigh over the open prairie in winter for more than ten miles were considered prohibitive. As a result numerous branch lines were built. With the development of excellent grid and main roads and the widespread use of motor trucks it is possible to haul grain much further with comparative ease. Many of the rural branch lines, moreover, were not high standard roads at any time. Some have not been properly maintained since they were built. As a result most branch and feeder rail lines cannot handle the new, heavier, and faster rolling stock now used by the railway companies. Many of the local delivery points are also too small to justify the employment of local agents, or to introduce new and more modern but often very expensive equipment. The economies of scale through the effective use of equipment and the volume necessary to justify new developments like large-unit-trains are simply not suited to the smaller delivery points on inadequate branch lines. Put simply, the grain-handling and transportation system is technologically obsolete and in need of modernization. Modernization, however, requires the abandonment of uneconomic branch lines and delivery points and the upgrading and improving of the larger centres. Such modernization is often bitterly resisted in rural areas. It is widely regarded as a threat to the survival of the much-vaunted family farm and the small prairie communities. Recognition and acceptance of the need for change is a prerequisite for any drastic overhaul and improvement of the western rail system. At present the inefficiencies of western operations increase rail costs and threaten to provide the railways with a better justification for their discriminatory rates than they have had at any time in the past.

The survival of rural life in Western Canada is directly affected by transportation costs. Clinging grimly to the remnants of the statutory Crow's Nest Pass rates and to inadequately maintained branch lines is no longer sufficient. Future farming costs will depend to a very large extent on the modernization and improvement of the existing grain-handling and transportation systems. The first requirement in any such overhaul should be an abandonment by the railways and by the Board of Railway Commissioners of the policy of "fair discrimination"—the policy of setting rates at low levels where competition exists and at much higher levels where water carriers cannot meet the needs of shippers.

Economic diversification and industrialization has become the objective of increasing numbers of Western Canadians. In order to facilitate this the discriminatory national freight-rate structure must be dismantled. The policy of "fair discrimination," modified by a few concessions to western grain farmers, is no longer adequate. What is needed is a genuine national transportation policy. Such a policy must encompass interregional rates which reflect equalization of rail service in much the same way that federal officials have found ways and means of equalizing fiscal resources, health services, education, unemployment insurance, pension schemes, and many other things between various regions. It should not, however, encompass transportation matters which are essentially matters of local or regional concern only. The subsidization of uneconomic local branch lines and the support of specific local industries or shippers are not proper concerns of the federal government. The responsibility of the federal government should be restricted to the provision of adequate, non-discriminatory main-line transportation facilities, sufficiently flexible to permit individual provinces to provide local subsidies if these are considered desirable locally or regionally. Almost all the prairie branch lines were originally incorporated and subsidized by provincial governments, not by the federal government. The relatively clear definition between national (i.e., main line) and provincial (i.e., local branch lines) which was worked out by the Laurier government between 1906 and 1910 needs to be re-established.[38]

The need for a non-discriminatory national transportation policy is obvious to Western Canadians. Unfortunately the federal position paper at the Western Economic Opportunities Conference indicates clearly that the old national rate-making philosophy based on competition or the lack of it is still alive and well in Ottawa. In the past, as has been shown, alterations in the national freight-rate structure which were regarded as indispensable to the development of Western Canada were achieved only when Western Canadians resorted to actions of their own, in defiance of national policies and of the rulings of the Board of Railway Commissioners. Manitoba created new and more competitive conditions by subsidizing and supporting new regional railways, thus forcing changes in national freight rates. Manitoba successfully meddled in national transportation policies, doing by indirect means what the federal government could have done by direct means. The problem was that the federal government would not act on its own. The real and permanent benefits obtained were obtained only because of Manitoba's actions.

The apparent federal reluctance to abandon the old rate-making philosophy makes it necessary for Western Canadians to once again consider aggressive action on their own. New and competitive regional railways would, of course, be inappropriate in an era of excessive regional rail capacity. Subsidization of alternate forms of transport, such as regional air lines and trucking systems, probably would prove far more effective. The railways and the Board of Transport Commissioners have great difficulty in understanding complaints about obvious discrimination, but they understand competition very well, whether that competition be real or artificial (i.e., from water carriers using government built and operated harbour and canal facilities).

There can be little doubt that subsidization of artificial competition is wasteful in most cases. It is nonetheless a very powerful weapon in forcing changes in federal policies which are unacceptable to one region of the country, but which seem insoluble through the usual channels of the federal system. Certainly western governments today could argue as forcefully as their predecessors did decades ago that the savings in reduced regional transportation costs would more than offset the provincial costs of subsidizing competition for the railways. The basic objective, of course, would be to create competition and reduce rates, not necessarily to transfer traffic from one carrier to another.

An alternative certainly open to wealthy provinces like Alberta would be to subsidize western shippers to the extent that the government believes the national railway rates discriminate against such shippers. Demands that money thus expended be taken into any calculations relating to federal-provincial finances or to equalization payments might well create a serious federal financial and constitutional problem. Federal-provincial financing arrangements and calculations would suffer for a time, but clearly greater regional pressure is needed to end nearly one hundred years of freight-rate discrimination.

Certainly unilateral action by one or more western governments to eliminate freight-rate discrimination is fraught with dangers. Not the least of these dangers is the disunity that might be created in Western Canada if freight-rate discrimination were eliminated. Western grain farmers now enjoy very considerable favourable discrimination under the Crow's Nest Pass Agreement and under the federal subsidization of rail operations on uneconomic branch lines. It is inconsistent and has often greatly weakened the western case when Westerners vehemently defend the Crow's Nest Pass rates or obsolete branch lines. On balance Western Canada has certainly suffered far more than it has gained from discriminatory freight rates, but a logical and united western position has often been difficult to achieve because of specific statutory concessions such as the Crow's Nest Pass rates.

Any coherent, logical, and determined action by one or more western provinces to eliminate freight-rate discrimination is likely to encounter legal, financial, and constitutional problems. The federal government probably has the power and the resources to defeat the policies of any province if it is willing to risk a complete rupture in its relations with that province and perhaps with an entire region. The experience of the past indicates that no federal government is likely, on its own initiative, to ameliorate or remove unpopular features of a policy which receives strong support in Central Canada, but is opposed in one or more minority regions. On the other hand, no federal government has been willing to thwart and nullify determined, well thought out, and sustained action by provincial governments in a minority region to remove major grievances. The challenge for Western Canadians is to devise a rational transportation policy and to take whatever action is necessary to achieve that policy. The Western Economic Opportunities Conference in July of 1973 demonstrated that the federal government can speak very sympathetically about western transportation problems, but has not yet abandoned the practice of setting rates according to differing degrees of competition.

Conclusion

National transportation policies certainly have been unduly burdensome to Western Canadians in the past. Those burdens have been ameliorated but not removed by the unilateral action of the province of Manitoba in the three decades after the incorporation of the Canadian Pacific Railway. The burden will only be further lightened if western politicians and spokesmen develop rational and more equitable alternative policies and insist on their implementation, through the federal process if possible, but through unilateral action if the parliament of Canada and the Canadian Transport Commission prove intransigent. Contradictory and carping criticism and complaints, or mendicant requests for make-shift subsidies, are no longer adequate. A well-defined and rational western transportation policy, backed by provincial governments willing and able to act on their own if necessary, offers the best and perhaps the only prospect for the easing of the burdens that national transportation policies have imposed on Western Canada.

NOTES

1. Western Economic Opportunities Conference, 24 to 26 July, 1973, Calgary, Alberta (hereafter referred to as W.E.O.C.), Background Paper on Transportation prepared by the Federal Government.
2. D.A. MacGibbon, *Railway Rates and the Canadian Railway Commission* (Boston, 1917), chap. III; R.A.C. Henry et al., *Railway Freight Rates in Canada: A Study Prepared for the Royal Commission on Dominion-Provincial Relations* (Ottawa, 1939). No reference will be made in this study to freight rates in the Maritime provinces. Those rates are the subject of a separate study in this book.
3. For an elaborate discussion and justification of western rates and the concept of "fair discrimination" see *Canadian Railway Cases,* Vol. 17, pp. 123-230, Western Tolls Case, Board of Railway Commissioners File No. 18755. The Board of Railway Commissioners in its judgment in the Western Tolls case acknowledged that "Prima facie discrimination in such tolls exists," but argued that this discrimination "is justified by effective water competition, and by the competition of U.S. railways throughout eastern Canada." Ibid., pp. 123-25.
4. Stephen to Macdonald, 27 August 1881, Macdonald Papers, Vol. 288, p. 121884, P.A.C.
5. Stephen to Macdonald, 13 November 1880, ibid., Vol. 268, p. 121844.
6. Stephen to Macdonald, 18 October 1880, ibid., p. 121836-37.
7. Chester Martin, *"Dominion Lands" Policy* (Toronto, 1973, reprint ed.), chap. II, "The Purposes of the Dominion."
8. MacGibbon, *Railway Rates,* chap. IV, "Results of the Canadian Transportation Policy."
9. Van Horne to E.B. Osler, 27 January 1883, Van Horne Letterbook No. 1, p. 211-12, P.A.C.
10. Aikins to Macdonald, 30 November 1883, Macdonald Papers, Vol. 186, pp. 77427-28; P.A.C. Van Horne to the Editor of the *Manitoba Free Press,* 24 December 1883, Van Horne Letterbook No. 4, pp. 12-13. P.A.C.
11. H.A. Innis, *History of the Canadian Pacific Railway* (Toronto, 1971, reprint ed.). Detailed operating statistics are given in chapters 7, 8, and 9.
12. *Canadian Railway Cases,* Vol. 17, p. 128.
13. William J. Wilgus, *The Railway Interrelationships of the United States and Canada* (New Haven, 1937).
14. *Canadian Railway Cases,* Vol. 17, p. 124, point 9.
15. W.E.O.C., Background Paper on Transportation prepared by the Federal Government.
16. Canada, *Debates of the House of Commons, 1883,* p. 971, Sir Charles Tupper on 4 May 1883. A more detailed discussion of the disallowance of Manitoba railway legislation is contained in J.A. Jackson, "Disallowance of Manitoba Railway Legislation in the 1880's; Railway Policy as a Factor in the Relations of Manitoba with the Dominion" (MA thesis, University of Manitoba, 1945); and T.D. Regehr, "The National Policy and Manitoba Railway Legislation, 1879-1888" (MA thesis, Carleton University, 1963).

17. Macdonald to McDougall, 30 July 1884, Macdonald Papers, Vol. 526, pp. 42-43. P.A.C.

18. Records of the Governor General's Office, Series G. 21, File 191, P.A.C.

19. W.B. Scarth to Macdonald, 5 May 1886, Macdonald Papers, Vol. 261, p. 119026-39. P.A.C.

20. Scarth to Macdonald and Macdonald to Scarth, 18 January 1887, and Scarth to Macdonald and Macdonald to Scarth, 2 February 1887, ibid., Vol. 262, pp. 119172, 119176, 119215.

21. Canada, *P.C. 577 of 1888* (Dormants), Final Memorandum respecting the visit of the delegation of the Manitoba government in reference to the disallowance of provincial legislation.

22. Lt. Col. Scoble to Greenway, 20 March 1888, Greenway Papers, Folio No. 283, Public Archives of Manitoba; Macdonald to Greenway, 30 March 1888, Macdonald Papers, Vol. 527, p. 458, P.A.C.

23. Villard Papers, Folder entitled "Northern Pacific and Manitoba Railway Company Testimony," Baker Library, Harvard Business School; Minnesota State Historical Society, *Northern Pacific Railroad Company Records,* Office of the Secretary, File 26, entitled "Northern Pacific and Manitoba Railway Company, 1888-1899." Both of these sources contain extensive evidence relating to the railway situation in Manitoba and the arrangement between the Northern Pacific Railroad and the Canadian Pacific Railway to avoid real competition.

24. A good discussion of the general background of the Crow's Nest Pass Agreement can be found in D.J. Hall, "The Political Career of Clifford Sifton, 1896-1905" (PH.D. thesis, University of Toronto, 1974).

25. Porteous to James Ross, 15 June 1897, Porteous Papers, Vol. 26, Letterbook, 1897-1898, p. 102; Porteous to Mackenzie, 29 June 1897, ibid., p. 119, P.A.C.

26. T.D. Regehr, *The Canadian Northern Railway: Pioneer Road of the Northern Prairies, 1895-1918,* (Toronto, 1976), chap. 3.

27. T.D. Regehr, "The Canadian Northern Railway: The West's Own Product," *Canadian Historical Review* (June 1970), p. 177-87.

28. Manitoba, *1Edw. VII, Cap. 39.*

29. Canada, *House of Commons Debates, 1901,* p. 5206.

30. *Canadian Railway Cases,* Vol. 22, pp. 4-49; Eastern Tolls Case, Board of Railway Commissioners File 25347. The difficulties of the new transcontinentals in operating their new lines north of Lake Superior are discussed in some detail in this case.

31. *Canadian Railway Cases,* Vol. 22, pp. 49-84; Increase in Passenger and Freight Tolls Case, Board of Railway Commissioners File 27840.

32. A.W. Currie, "Freight Rates on Grain in Western Canada," *Canadian Historical Review,* (March 1940), pp. 40-55.

33. W.E.O.C., "Transportation" (position paper jointly submitted by Premiers Allan Blakeney, David Barrett, Edward Schreyer, and Peter Lougheed).

34. W.E.O.C., Document, Jean Marchand to Hon. E.J. Benson, President, Canadian Transportation Commission, 19 July 1973.

33. Ibid.
36. John Channon, Section Three, Paper five, in *Grain Handling and Transportation Seminar,* held 8 and 9 March 1973, Saskatoon, Saskatchewan. Proceedings published by the Canada Grains Council and the University of Saskatchewan.
37. All these issues and problems have been discussed repeatedly. The Grain Handling and Transportation Seminar focused on many of these issues.
38. For an interesting and thoughtful approach to the problem see J. Donal Howe, "The Possible Railroad: Towards a New Transport Policy," *Canadian Forum* (February 1974), pp. 4-10.

DAVID E. SMITH

Western Politics and National Unity

There is nothing unusual in the benefits of a federation being unequally distributed among its constituent units—it happens in all existing federations and contributed to the disintegration of several that failed (i.e., the West Indies and Malaysia). But as a rule, in a federal polity the least-favoured areas are the seat of the greatest resentment. What is unusual in Canada is that the four western provinces, who are materially better off than the five eastern provinces, and two of whom rival Ontario in per-capita wealth, should be marked by a long history of anti-federal sentiment. Moreover, on the prairies, political action accompanied dissent. This has manifested itself most visibly in support given, first, to new parties, and, later, to the major federal opposition party. Unlike the residents of Quebec, with whom Westerners have shared some grievances, prairie voters have in recent years effectively excluded themselves and their region from the ranks of the governing Liberal party.[1] This collective rejection of the dominant party of this century in federal politics has in turn exacerbated the region's sense of isolation.

To the outsider, the legacy of Western Canadian resentment of the federal government is mystifying. In the eyes of the resident of Ontario, the West, in the energy-conscious seventies, is both economically and politically potent. For Quebeckers, the region constitutes a significant part of English Canada's dominant majority. Indeed, they view it as the hostile heartland of anti-French feeling. And to the envious Easterner, the western provinces, even "have-not" Manitoba, share a material prosperity never found in the Atlantic region.

The continuing disaffection of the West is the result of no single factor but stems from grievances that are economic, political, and even cultural in origin. If there is one element common to each, however, it might be termed "unfulfilled expectations." The prairie West (which is the subject of this paper) at the opening of the twentieth century was a land of superlatives. When its great potential went unrealized, frustration, not doubt, replaced optimism. On the prairies there was never any question but that the region's promise was thwarted by federal policies that alternated between neglect and exploitation. Most recently, after a decade of singular devotion to Quebec's problems, the federal government is viewed from the prairies, in the conflict over oil and natural gas, as once again turning its guns and not its ear to the West.

Roots of Dissent: Economic
The economic grievances of the prairies have arisen from the role assigned them by several generations of federal policymakers. For most of this century, Westerners generally accepted their designated place as primary, especially wheat, producers but rejected the restrictive conditions under which they were expected to function. In recent years, however, prairie residents and their governments have begun to press for new federal policies that would allow them to diversify their single-crop economy. Three Farmers' Platforms, adopted in 1910, 1916, and 1920 by the Canadian Council of Agriculture, and virtually every statement made by a western politician before the depression, demanded lower tariffs (preferably free trade in natural products with the United States), more equitable freight rates, government operation of terminal elevators, and a government-owned and operated Hudson Bay Railway.[2] The platform of 1921 and the Progressive party's stand during its years in the House of Commons demonstrated an additional concern for good government, more particularly the reform of institutions like the Senate and the electoral system, which were viewed as iniquitous. But it was trade and transportation, as it affected the

region's and the nation's major crop—wheat—that aroused the West.

Policies that would lower the cost of growing wheat were necessary, it was argued, if prairie farmers were to be encouraged to stay on the land. And that, the Farmers' platform of 1910 said, was what they should do, because "the greatest misfortune which can befall any country is to have its people huddled together in great centres of population."[3] Two decades later, this anti-metropolitan sentiment was echoed by Conservatives in Saskatchewan who feared Anglo-Saxon farmers would lead the exodus to the cities if conditions did not improve, and leave the countryside to the foreigner.[4] Concern for maintaining the family farm, about which so much is heard today, only assumed prominence when the mechanization of agriculture made it an endangered institution after the Second World War.[5]

The demands of the western farmer before the First World War generally received a sympathetic hearing by the federal governments of the day. As difficult as that may be for Westerners to believe now, the explanation then made good economic sense. According to Vernon Fowke, there was a tremendous national investment in the wheat economy that had to be protected:

The prospect for the profitable employment of capital and labour in the production of wheat on the Canadian plains attracted millions of immigrants to the continent and to the region, and prompted the investment of billions of dollars not only in the prairie provinces but throughout the entire nation. The prairie provinces constituted the geographic locus of the Canadian investment frontier in the first three decades of the twentieth century . . . .

An investment frontier may be geographically diffused but it nevertheless has tangible, concrete expression in the process of real-capital formation. The establishment of the wheat economy required the assembly in the prairie provinces of a massive structure of capital equipment without which the large-scale production and marketing of wheat would have been impossible. This included not only the equipment of the farms but also the equally indispensable equipment of the market centres throughout the region and of the transportation routes between.[6]

Gradually, at agrarian urging, the federal government assumed responsibility for the inspection, quality, transportation, and (in some instances) storage of prairie wheat. But federal intervention on behalf of the farmers was as much the result of Ottawa's calculation of the national interest as it was a victory for agrarian pressure politics. It should be remembered that "all parts of the Dominion with the exception of the maritime provinces expanded their industrial and other economic activity in direct response to the opening of the prairie market."[7]

Both of the federal parties appreciated the need to secure the wheat economy, but the Liberals in 1911, with their stronger agrarian but weaker business ties, were willing to go further than the Conservatives. They pledged themselves to reciprocity with the United States. Although manufactured goods were not included, the proposal was feared and fought by commercial groups as the first step to economic union of the two countries. For the Tories, the wheat economy had made the dream of a successful national economic policy a reality. Reciprocity, they believed, would enrich western wheat farmers but at the expense of Central Canadian industrialists. When the naval issue weakened Laurier's support in Quebec, the Liberals could not carry reciprocity—identified as it was with the interests of the West—on western support alone. In the 1911 campaign the interests of three of Canada's regions were directly in conflict, but when the votes were counted, only those of one—Ontario—had been satisfied. The effects of the failure to secure reciprocity with the United States can be overemphasized. Had the agreement been achieved, it would have moderated but not removed western dissent. The other grievances—freight rates and elevators—would have remained, and its defeat did not bring an immediate agrarian revolt. The years before the war were a time of expansion and the war itself buoyed the wheat economy. Indeed, the federal government, using its emergency power under the War Measures Act in 1919, created an extremely popular but short-lived wheat board whose restoration became the elusive goal of the next generation of farmers.[8]

It was the adjustment to peacetime that definitely marked an end to the period of uninterrupted growth that had existed on the prairies since the opening of the century. From the appearance of the Progressives as a political force in 1920 until the creation of the Canadian Wheat Board in 1935, the western farmers fought for better treatment on several fronts. Initially, they pressed the federal government to create a peacetime wheat board with the same broad powers to set prices as enjoyed by its "wartime" predecessor. But court decisions after the war denied to the federal government the sole constitutional authority to act. The best Ottawa could do was create a board that required supplementary legislation on the part of two or more prairie provinces to endow it with powers comparable to the old one. Nevertheless, Manitoba never acted and the other two provinces failed to find sufficient personnel. By the mid-twenties, in any case, interest in a wheat board waned as farmers were caught up in the crusade for a voluntary wheat pool. The pool was based on the principle of cooperation which was much respected and practised on the prairies. Farmers who signed five-year contracts with the pool were committed to sell all the grain they produced through its facilities. The story of the pool's success and then collapse in 1931 has been told before and is not relevant here, except to note that while it operated, wheat ceased to be a subject of political friction.[9] With wheat removed from politics and the economy prosperous, regional dissent was minimal.

One sign of a return to something approaching prewar harmony was the decline of the Progressive party. The number of prairie seats in the House of Commons increased from forty-three in 1921 to fifty-four in 1926 but the number of Progressive members declined from thirty-eight to eighteen. The government of W. L. Mackenzie King, after an uncertain beginning, had managed to placate prairie critics and undermine the Progressive revolt. The tariff, against which Westerners of all partisan stripes had railed, was reduced in 1924. The same year the old Crow's Nest Pass rates, which guaranteed reduced freight charges on grain and certain other commodities and which had been suspended in 1918 under authority of the War Measures Act, were restored.[10]

The transfer of natural resources to the prairie provinces by Ottawa in 1930 was interpreted in the West as the final step in achieving provincial autonomy. Retention of the resources by the federal government in 1870 and 1905 had acted as a continual irritant in federal – provincial relations even though, in the case of Saskatchewan and Alberta, the financial settlement in lieu of resources had been generous. Ironically the year 1930 did not inaugurate a period of prosperity on the prairies, with the provinces using the resources to further their individual development, but was, instead, the beginning of depression and drought that were to destroy the prairie economy. Rather than a decade in which the region began to loosen its ties to the centre, the thirties witnessed first collapse and then total dependency of the three prairie provinces upon Ottawa. According to the Rowell-Sirois Report, Saskatchewan, Alberta, and Manitoba (in that order) led the provinces of Canada in the decline of provincial per-capita incomes between 1928-29 and 1933.[11]

The single most important policy development of the thirties, as it affected the prairie provinces then and later, was the creation in 1935 of the Canadian Wheat Board. By this action, the federal government began a course that would eventually lead it to assume sole responsibility for the orderly marketing of wheat. The political ramifications of this decision and its contribution to regional dissent became apparent only over time. Wheat was no longer de-politicized, as it had been in the period of the pools, but neither was it open to legislative manipulation as in the prewar years. The provinces were now free to criticize the federal government's policies towards the board, while the board was generally free of federal government intervention in its activities. In this triangular relationship of board, farmer, and federal government, the government appeared vulnerable. For the board there was a reservoir of good will among farmers that grew from memories of the high wheat prices of 1917 through 1920 when grain had previously been controlled by a wheat board. But the farmers were congenitally suspicious of the government.

For nearly twenty years the new system worked well. The farmers were happy with the good, stabilized prices the board secured for them and the federal government took the credit. But if their wheat policy brought acclaim to the Liberals it also, eventually, brought criticism. The massive harvests of the fifties which saw the volume of farm-stored wheat triple created a problem that price stabilization could not solve. The Liberals' answer to the wheat glut was to have the farmers bear the storage charges, aided by low-interest loans. The board was the responsibility of C. D. Howe, minister of trade and commerce. His reputation for business acumen rang hollow to farmers when wheat sales declined and he refused to consider any but hard currency, non-Communist customers. His reputation for arrogance struck home when he threatened to withdraw the low-interest-loan legislation if opposition members of Parliament delayed its passage by criticizing its terms.[12]

More than any other single issue, the government's wheat policies were responsible for its loss of support on the prairies in 1957. The Liberals won only six of forty-eight seats, down eleven from 1953. Wheat delivered the region to the Progressive Conservatives and has held it for them. In its first session of Parliament, the Diefenbaker government introduced the Prairie Grain Advance Payments Act which provided advance payment to producers for grain in storage, a policy the Liberals had refused to initiate.[13] Large grain sales to Communist countries followed and the Progressive Conservatives "ingratiated [themselves] with thousands of electors."[14] Between 1958 and 1974, there were 327 constituency contests in general elections on the prairies and the Tories won 267 of them. Of the remaining 60, the Liberals won only 25.

The policies that proved so electorally successful for the Progressive Conservatives preserved the institution of the Canadian Wheat Board as it had operated during the Liberal hegemony of 1935 to 1957. The wheat glut, and its resulting storage problems of the 1950s, was a technical question that was eliminated by moving wheat. The first substantive policies to alter the western grains industry appeared only in the late 1960s during the Trudeau government. These policies, which have been identified with the minister responsible for the Wheat Board, Otto Lang, have included a program to reduce wheat stocks and diversify western agriculture (Lower Inventories for Tomorrow), a grain income stabilization plan, and removal of feed grains from the Wheat Board's control. Each of these ideas, along with a suggestion that the Crow's Nest Pass rates be reexamined, has been received with alarm on the prairies and has had to be amended, withdrawn, or curtailed.

The evolution of Canada's wheat economy, especially the federal government's assumption of responsibility through the creation and operation of a wheat board, has increased regional dissent. The board and the institutions and policies that surround it have come to possess an aura of sanctity that deters change or even suggestions of change. Distrust and suspicion of those who propose reforms, especially when they are in the central government, are heightened when the Liberal party is in power. That party has deteriorated as a political force in Western Canada at the same time as its hold on the central region of the country has increased. Changing party fortunes have made the Liberal party's few prairie members appear unrepresentative of the West. By contrast, the Progressive Conservative party seems unable (and, in truth, at times unwilling) to divest itself of its western "image." The detrimental effect of this alignment upon national policy is obvious, but equally damaging is its implication for regional policies which have to be negotiated or extorted, not developed in "a spirit of cooperation."

The experience of the prairie provinces in the last decade, as they have sought to diversify their economies, testifies to the absence of harmony in the relationship between the West and Ottawa (especially Liberal Ottawa). Some of the most bitter obloquy was voiced by Saskatchewan Liberals, in power between 1964 and 1971, led by W. Ross Thatcher. Unlike their N.D.P. opponents, who favoured state direction and control, Thatcher's Liberals were committed, at least publicly, to an unplanned private enterprise economy. And, like the classic entrepreneur, they sought to spread benefits and risks among as many investors and businessmen as possible. Saskatchewan's natural resources were the province's major attraction and Thatcher soon found himself locked in combat with the federal Liberals over policies to develop them. The premier never accepted the priority given in the sixties to constitutional reform by Pearson and later Trudeau. Financial problems, he said, were "the major challenge to the continued existence of our country."[15] He was particularly incensed by the federal government's white paper on taxation, issued in 1969, which he described as "the most damnable piece of legislation" he had seen since becoming a Liberal.[16] The Saskatchewan government attacked the cancellation of exemptions previously enjoyed by mining companies on the ground that it would discourage new mining ventures in the West at a time when Saskatchewan desired just such investment.

But Thatcher was not alone in his criticism and rejection of national policies. The recent debate, between Saskatchewan and Alberta on the one hand, and Ottawa and the rest of the provinces on the other, over the use and cost of energy resources and the Saskatchewan government's decision, late in 1975, to nationalize the potash industry (while the constitutionality of its resource taxation policy was still before the courts) is evidence of the continuing conflict that has marked the economic history of the prairie provinces. These events confirm in the minds of Westerners the image they have of an "imperial" federal government which, when the need arises, will sacrifice their interests and patrimony in the name of national unity but, in reality, for the good of Central Canada. This is the distribution of power that Westerners believe exists. Any other interpretation they believe to be window-dressing, including the prime minister's plea to the Western Economic Opportunities Conference in 1973, "for a new approach to national development wherein our goal must be to seek balanced and diversified regional economies across the country."[17] At the conference, the four western provinces sought changes in federal policies (as they affected the region's agriculture, economic and industrial development, transportation, and financial institutions). The lack of progress since belies Trudeau's claim that "it is no longer essential for our survival to think of a single industrial heartland and a resource-based perimeter."[18]

Roots of Dissent: Politics
The dissent found in Western Canada today stems almost as much from grievances that arise out of its political culture as it does from economic unrest. Here, because of a singular combination of events among which must be numbered the influx of an ethnically heterogeneous population settling on homesteads spread over thousands of square miles where services were

expensive and attainable only through local initiative, a unique set of attitudes, beliefs, values, and skills developed. Consider the place of cooperatives, which, from the great provincial elevator companies to the village store, were a pillar of the prairie community; or the interrelationship of politics and religion as witnessed in the Social Gospel of T. C. Douglas and J. S. Woodsworth or the Social Credit of William Aberhart. The prairie experience with both has no Canadian equivalent. Nor is labour's turbulent history in the West duplicated elsewhere in Canada, although of course this is no measure of its respective import for the nation's history. At the same time, although the prairie provinces share a regional political culture, each of them can claim its own distinctive set of characteristics. It is this very pluralism which explains the region's rich heritage of protest.

Politics, in the form of party, movement, and pressure groups, has been both an expression and a cause of western dissent. Until the end of the First World War, when the Progressives burst upon the federal scene and the farmers captured power in Winnipeg and Edmonton, the politics and parties of the prairie provinces were an integral part of the national political structure. Regional dissent, as seen in the Farmers' platform of 1910 and 1916, was expressed either through pressure-group activity or through one of the two original national parties. Western farmers had established their provincial organizations (the United Farmers of Manitoba, the United Farmers of Alberta, and the Saskatchewan Grain Growers' Association) early in the history of their respective provinces and these bodies quickly assumed a powerful position in provincial politics as well as an articulate and united voice in the federated Canadian Council of Agriculture. Pressure-group activity in this period succeeded because governments at both the federal and provincial levels responded to the demands of the developing West. In the conflict of interests which is the hallmark of politics and the raison d'être of federalism, the West and its farmers lost only one major battle—reciprocity in 1911. The old party structure helped simplify the job of the pressure groups. As long as there were Liberals or Conservatives in power in Ottawa and in the provinces, grievances could be transmitted directly through the partisan pipeline. From local constituency officials through to the federal cabinet minister, who was the acknowledged spokesman for the province in the national capital, provincial and federal parties (this distinction is itself misleading since it was not made at the time) sought to serve one another.

Before 1921, integration of the federal political system developed through reciprocal support of each level's policies as well as politicians primarily because the major federal programs of interest to the West concerned the development of the wheat economy. But other federal policies, whatever their subject, were bound to evoke response from provincial politicians; then too the federal party dichotomy was not, as C. B. Macpherson has argued, "extraneous" to Alberta and the other prairie provinces.[19] Even if prairie society was overwhelmingly petit bourgeois, as Macpherson contends, parties were not solely mediators of class conflict. There were other issues where national parties took positions which had nothing to do with class conflict but on which prairie parties and voters were forced to align themselves. One example concerned religion and education. Manitoba's politics had been thrown into turmoil in the 1890s by legislation, considered by some to be a violation of the spirit of its terms of union, to create a public school system that did not provide denominational schools for Roman Catholics. Despite a partial compromise that quelled some passions, Manitoba's government got what it wanted. Yet the issue was not laid to rest and continued to reassert itself provincially into the 1960s. In Alberta and Saskatchewan, a similar dispute arose in 1905 when it appeared that the autonomy legislation would extend denominational rights in education beyond former territorial practice. There had been little acrimony over separate schools in the Territories but the events of 1905 injected a degree of emotion to the subject that abated only slightly after the Laurier government removed the offending clause. A cleavage had been formed in provincial politics where none existed before. It assumed increased prominence, especially in Saskatchewan, during the First World War as a result of jingoistic campaigns against foreigners (many of whom were Roman Catholic) and at the end of the twenties due to the abuse of the immigrant by the Ku Klux Klan.[20]

Integration of the parties on both levels of government was irremediably damaged in 1917 with the creation of the Union government led by Sir Robert Borden. Except at its birth, that government, which included the minister responsible for the successful Liberal party organization in Saskatchewan (J. A. Calder) and the Liberal premier of Alberta (Arthur Sifton), was viewed in the West as essentially Tory in complexion and therefore hostile in design. The political significance of this judgment may be better appreciated in company with the returns of the four federal elections between 1900 and 1911: in the area between Ontario and British Columbia the Liberals won fifty-four of the eighty-six seats at stake. But coalition also indicated partisanship generally because its calculated disregard of past politics strengthened those critics of the system whose fortunes had waxed and waned since the turn of the century. Liberals and Conservatives were never so entrenched on the prairies that they could afford to forget the original non-partisan base of territorial politics or ignore the periodic threat of groups like the Non-Partisan League who challenged the utility, as well as ethics, of partisan politics.[21]

The temporary eclipse of prairie Grits in parliament opened the way for disillusioned Westerners in the House of Commons to coalesce in a new Progressive party. Although the Progressives attracted much attention in 1921 when they demanded a new national policy and won thirty-eight of the prairie provinces' forty-three seats, they were essentially reformist Liberals whose momentum was halted when the Liberals, under Mackenzie King, adopted some planks in their platform and co-opted their first two leaders, T. A. Crerar and Robert Forke.

Because both their accomplishments and failures are so ambiguous, the place of the Progressives in Canadian political history remains enigmatic.[22] Their legislative record, in terms of policies successfully carried through parliament, was meagre. Depending on the observer's partisan leanings, the Progressives were either the taskmaster or handmaiden of Liberal politicians, some of whom saw the new party as a retribution for their indiscretion with Borden's Tories. The Progressives were not a protest party of the West only—over 41 per cent of the victories in 1921 were outside of the prairies (mainly in

Ontario). In addition to its prairie strength as "a sectional protest against a metropolitan economy, it was also [on the prairies as elsewhere] an agrarian protest against the growing urban domination of the Canadian economy and of national politics."[23] For the Westerner, the Progressive movement offered an opportunity to repudiate those economic terms of Confederation that made the region a captive of the centre and which were aggravated by postwar inflation for all commodities except wheat, whose average annual price fell from $2.51 a bushel (as set by the temporary wheat board) in 1920 to $1.65 (on the open market) in 1921.[24] Eastern as well as western Progressives opposed the transformation of Canada from a rural-agricultural to an urban-industrial society. Anti-metropolitan sentiment, heightened by further growth of the large cities during the war, had been evident for some time, even on the prairies which were the least urban of Canada's regions.

The Progressives failed to reverse the forces against which they protested just as they failed to secure most of the legislation they promoted. Yet their short-lived revolt was significant for subsequent protest groups in Western Canada. First, it stimulated the provincial farmers' associations to consider entering politics directly as electoral organizations. The United Farmers of Alberta in 1919 and the United Farmers of Manitoba by 1922 decided to follow the federal Progressives' example, to the extent that the organized farmers in both provinces deserted the old parties. Once into electoral politics, the theory of group government set the Alberta farmers apart from their brothers elsewhere, but the effect of that initial decision was as disruptive for traditional parties there as in other provinces.[25]

The farmers of Saskatchewan, organized in the Saskatchewan Grain Growers' Association, made a hesitant entry into provincial politics in 1922 but reversed their decision two years later. This agrarian indecision was the result of the Liberal party's success since 1905 at co-opting prominent leaders and advocating popular policies with a critical eye for simple solutions. When Saskatchewan farmers wanted public ownership of elevators, as in Manitoba, the government responded with legislation to promote cooperatives, and when the Non-Partisan League's cry for cheap money was echoed by "responsible" farmers, the province's Liberals provided long-term, low-interest loans. The Saskatchewan Co-operative Elevator Company and the Farm Loan Board were among the most popular and financially successful enterprises that Saskatchewan Liberal governments ever introduced. Thus, during the twenties, Saskatchewan's politics and parties survived the farmers' revolt, while in Alberta and Manitoba, the old party systems were destroyed. The Liberals, who had held power in Edmonton ever since the province was created, were displaced and never returned while in Winnipeg the success of the U.F.M. initiated an era of non-partisan and then coalition government that was to last for thirty-five years. Rebellion against the traditional party alignment thus loosened the bonds of Confederation by increasing the opportunities for regional dissent.

The Progressives influenced the course of western protest in a second, but this time negative, way. Both Social Credit and C.C.F. enthusiasts considered the old Progressive revolt ineffectual, although each learned a different lesson from the episode. Social Credit, like the U.F.A. before it, distrusted brokerage politics and interpreted the Progressives' fate as confirmation of the danger inherent in cooperation. The C.C.F., however, sought cooperation with other groups (but not the Communists) and blamed the Progressives' weaknesses on poor organization, a failing the C.C.F. never displayed. This, however, was the extent of the connection between the Progressives and these later protest movements. Some Progressives, it is true, did join Social Credit or the C.C.F. but many more returned to the Liberal party from whence they had come.[26]

Social Credit and the C.C.F. represented a new form of dissent. W. L. Morton describes them (particularly Social Credit) as "Utopian" in the sense that they sought "to merge the nation in the section."[27] Unlike the Progressives, who wanted to reform the existing economic and political system, the new parties each sought to replace the old order with one constructed according to new principles. At its English inception, Social Credit was an economic theory that saw politics as a means to attain a goal, but later, in Alberta, because of the Canadian constitution, this idea was abandoned. Social Credit quickly emerged as a regional protest party whose political ambitions led it to clash most resoundingly with Mackenzie King and his Liberals and with the federal government and its offspring, the Rowell-Sirois Commission.

Because of its socialist doctrine and diverse origins, the C.C.F. was never a regional party like Social Credit. In Saskatchewan, the strong base provided by the United Farmers of Canada (Saskatchewan Section) and the eventual victory of the C.C.F. over the ruling provincial Liberals gave the new party an agrarian aura. Yet its urban-industrial supporters always exerted great influence in the party's organization. The achievement of the C.C.F. and its successor, the New Democratic Party, was the revolution it wrought in political and social thought after the Regina Manifesto—governments and individuals today accept as reasonable many of the movement's principles. But this national success deprived the party of any special claim to representing regional interests, particularly those of the West. Even in its Saskatchewan bastion, the assertion could never be supported by electoral results. In the period between 1935 and 1957 (including the elections of those years), 117 federal seats were contested in the province and the Liberals won fifty-three to the C.C.F.'S fifty-one. The Progressive Conservatives won nine and other candidates four.

By the early fifties, the protest parties of the West had become "provincialized." Prairie voters who wanted to vent their wrath at Liberals and who also hoped to change government policies had to look elsewhere. Eventually they focused on the one party that had never been popular in the West, the Progressive Conservatives. In the fifty years before 1958, the party had won only 22 per cent of prairie seats at stake in general elections. This, however, increased to 81 per cent of the region's seats in the period 1958 through 1974. It was a dramatic swing in partisan sympathy and is all the more remarkable because of its apparent permanence. Equally impressive, however, has been the rejection of the Liberals in all three provinces. Only in Quebec is there a similar alignment of the old parties, although there it is the Progressive Conservatives who are unpopular.

The Tories' success in the West is not the subject of this paper except as it is interpreted to be a continuation of the tradition of prairie political protest. With the passing of each recent general election, the hold of the Progessive Conservatives upon the region becomes more notable. Neither the competence nor record of the Diefenbaker government can explain it. It is, rather, a dissentient vote directed against the centre and the Liberal party, which today is identified with the centre. Western Progressive Conservatives are generally more Progressive than Conservative. They articulate the same values and interest that supporters of the Progressive, Social Credit, and c.c.f. parties once did. This "floating" protest vote has been attracted, at different times, to different parties which have almost always been in opposition in Ottawa. Nothing reveals more accurately the political impotence of the region or the lack of hope for improvement. The burden of unity, which the West believes it has borne for so long, will lighten only if the region can secure policies more favorable to itself. For this to happen, the West must secure a greater voice at the centre in federal decisions or it must have more autonomy to formulate its own policies.

The First Alternative

A great voice at the centre requires, in effect, more participation by Westerners in the deliberations of the Liberal party. Because there is only a handful of Liberals to represent the West's interests, Liberal governments have generally been unreceptive to the region's demands and, even when sympathetic, unable to carry legislation through because of lack of popular or parliamentary support. There are ways in which the current situation could change. Western voters could elect more Liberals which, in light of the party's national electoral success, would be reasonable. But given the region's recent voting preferences this is unlikely. An alternative would be to reform the electoral system so that the Liberals' popular vote (which, as a proportion of the party's national vote, has ranged in the last fifteen years from a low of 10 per cent in 1974 to a high of 13 per cent in 1968) would be translated more accurately into elected members (which, as the proportion of the party's seats in parliament, have ranged in the same period from 2 per cent in 1962 to 7 per cent in 1968). Reform of the electoral system is scarcely discussed in Canada except in isolated instances, such as in Quebec by Parti Québécois supporters after the last provincial election. Nevertheless, the fact remains that the absence of strong western representation in recent Liberal governments explains the party's plight in the West. It is also clear that without a vocal expression of concern for the West's interests in caucus and in support of the few prairie ministers who do speak for the region, the area's concerns receive relatively low priority. One may argue about the comparative impact of caucus, cabinet, and the senior civil service upon the formulation of policy but low visibility in at least two of these key areas effectively mutes the prairies' voice.[28]

A political party is more than an electoral organization, even though that is its principal function for the Liberals and Progressive Conservatives. One of the jobs of a party is to act as a transmission belt, alternatively conveying constituency matters to the legislator and governmental policy to local supporters. The role of the riding association therefore becomes extremely important for it is continually required to evaluate interests and, in the first instance, legitimize government policy which, when found acceptable, is propagated and defended by the party faithful to the electorate. One of the Liberal party's greatest weaknesses in the West today is that the local organization is so often absent, atrophied, or suspicious of federal attachments.[29] Instead of audiences that are critical but ultimately concerned about the party, ministers frequently find themselves having to explain government policy to hostile interest groups. Repeated Progressive Conservative electoral sweeps have discouraged all but the truest prairie Grits who usually persevere because of personal motives that include, among others, ideology and hope for a share of federal patronage. The work of the local associations in promoting the party has increasingly been taken over by "communications specialists" who have substituted public relations for partisanship.

A striking contrast between federal Liberal governments since 1963 and their predecessors of a quarter of a century ago is the absence of dominant provincial spokesmen. The change is particularly noticeable to a Westerner because, as recently as the King and St. Laurent periods, J. G. Gardiner and Stuart Garson acted like barons whose authority in matters affecting their provinces was absolute. Today there is no minister of similar political stature. The tradition of co-opting prominent provincial politicians was not begun by King, nor was it unique to the Liberal party: Laurier invited three provincial premiers into his 1896 cabinet and Borden searched for regional talent especially for his Union government. As it affected Saskatchewan, however, the practice was particularly marked. Indeed, until 1971, all but one (W. J. Patterson) of eight provincial Liberal leaders sat in parliament at some point during their public careers.[30] Co-optation did not signify provincial party subservience nor ministerial parochialism. The party mobilized provincial grievances which the minister could vent in cabinet. At the same time, and perhaps more important in terms of promoting unity, the ministers acknowledged the importance of national policies through their continuing allegiance and participation.

Co-optation, which was one manifestation of what is now referred to as "elite accommodation," declined in significance for several reasons.[31] Although the Progressive Conservatives practised it, they were never as good at it as the Liberals, partly because there were fewer Progressive Conservative governments to draw from, as Diefenbaker discovered when he became prime minister. The evolution in federal-provincial relations of the last two decades has enhanced the status of provincial governments and made their politicians, of all stripes, less malleable to federal direction. But the principal reason for the decline of co-optation was the Liberal party's abandonment of the practice.

Even before the Diefenbaker era opened, Liberal party strength on the prairies had begun to decline. When the demands of the burgeoning urban middle-class electorate of southern Ontario captured the party's attention after the Second World War, the western voter felt ignored. In the aftermath of 1958, the regionalization of the party was intensified with the Liberals of Central Canada coming to dominate its councils. In an attempt to restore the party, they set out to refurbish its image, rebuild its organization, and reform its practices. Professing as their goal the greatest participation by the greatest number, they created federally appointed organizations to promote the interests of the federal party in each province. The first casualties of this innovation (as indeed was its intent) were the old provincial war-horses who had dominated the region's politics.

These changes, which were far more sweeping than this brief reference suggests, caused the Liberals special problems in the West where their hold was precarious in any case. On principle, the local faithful resented what they interpreted as dictation from the centre, while in practice they fought to maintain their traditional voice in patronage distribution. Internecine squabbles between federal and provincial Liberals, most of whom had never won an election, broke out in Alberta and Manitoba. In Saskatchewan, rancour spread between Thatcher and his supporters, who believed they should have a share of federal patronage, and the Ottawa loyalists, who viewed the methods and style of the new premier as quintessential "old politics." Seized by a desire to control the party, each camp of Liberals in Saskatchewan did little else than fight the other, while "those who believe[d] that policy had some importance . . . stay[ed] away from any meeting that sound[ed] organizational."[32]

The strategy of the sixties dictated that the Liberals should direct their appeal to where most of the voters lived. In fact, this tactic garnered votes in Ontario and, in turn, sharpened the party's metropolitan image. The isolated urban support it received on the prairies, where the few seats won were in the major cities, strengthened this impression. The absence of rural members made the Liberals appear the least representative party in the region. Representation is a notoriously slippery concept open to varied interpretation and, the theory of group government aside, there is no logical reason why farmers must represent farmers for agriculture to secure the legislation it wants or deserves. The fact remains, however, that although only the Liberal party can offer the prairies access to federal policy-making, it has failed to make its case. The old conflict between region and nation thus remains unresolved, even heightened. For the party, no obvious escape exists from the impasse, but for the region there is another option.

The Second Alternative
In the Canadian political system, where policy is the preserve of ministers and their advisers, the individual M.P., especially an opposition member, has few opportunities to influence its formulation. Thus a region of the country that withholds support from the government cannot realistically expect parliament to accommodate its interests. As an alternative, it must lay claim, on its own behalf, to a broader range of powers and control than has been customary in Canadian federalism.

All provinces in one way or another have done this in recent years as they have raised their sights and finances. Indeed, this collegial assertiveness has transformed traditional federal-provincial relations into quasi-diplomatic negotiations.[33] While no division of jurisdiction or of institutions in a federal system is immutable, any province or group of provinces seeking a redistribution of power must recognize that federalism is based on the existence of rival sovereign powers. Thus a proposal to alter the status quo necessarily requires adjustments and counteradjustments on the part of both levels of government. And, in the context of this discussion of alternatives, suggestions which have, as their ultimate goal, the extension of a province's or region's control of its development will inevitably be viewed as threatening by the federal government. The proposals must therefore be realistic in terms of their objectives and method of implementation. Otherwise they will be rejected both by Ottawa, which will view them as damaging to the political system, and by prairie residents, who are not "Rupert's Land nationalists" seeking hinterland independence.

Westerners view themselves as Canadians, maybe even "ideal" Canadians who, if left to their own devices, would ignore the myths and prejudices that obsess their eastern compatriots. In many respects, the West was never an extension of Central Canada except perhaps in its very earliest settlements. Later, it was a new land for hundreds of thousands of foreign immigrants ignorant of the passions of Canada's history. Yet, as creatures of the federal government, the prairies' political and economic development was tied closely to events at the centre. The West was made the testing ground for Confederation and the patronizing attitude that underlay this assumption stimulated resentment as much as any specific program—be it for tariffs or freight rates, bilingualism or energy policies.

The prairie provinces distrust the federal government, especially now that they have so little influence on its policies. The West has, to a large degree, achieved political autonomy in that the fortunes of its parties and politicians are nearly free of federal entanglements. In federal-provincial negotiations the prairie premiers, regardless of party, share to a remarkable degree interests that are essentially regional in scope. The Western Economic Opportunities Conference in July 1973, when the premiers of the four provinces west of Ontario prepared joint statements on a range of subjects, constituted the clearest evidence of this mutual concern.

Of course it is obvious that the problems confronting each province are not the same. Alberta's prosperity and growth, for instance, require a different set of policies from those needed to check the population decline and economic stagnation of Saskatchewan and Manitoba. When one speaks of the West, therefore, it does make a difference which province is being discussed. There is, nonetheless, sufficient common ground among the provinces in their disagreements with Ottawa to encourage three suggestions for change in the operation of the federal system. They are policies that would promote, first, decentralization, second, devolution, and, third, control.

Decentralization implies a transfer of federal instrumentalities to the region. Several possibilities exist. At the most visible level would be the establishment of local offices of major federal departments like Agriculture and Regional Economic Expansion, large proportions of whose clientele live in the region. The purpose of this proposal quite simply is to give broader access to and thus encourage more local participation in the making and carrying out of those federal governmental policies of special importance to the prairies. Decentralization of another sort (which has actually begun in limited areas) is to move federal enterprises like the Royal Canadian Mint and Air Canada's overhaul base to the West. As an indication of federal commitment to redress a policy of neglect, such actions are commendable. They are not welcome as token gestures. The ultimate purpose of such developments must be to generate skills and talents, not just jobs.

One of the significant contrasts between Canada and the United States is the continuing unrivalled dominance of a few large old cities here and the growth of regional "technological" centres (Detroit after the First World War, and Houston, Kansas City, and Seattle after the Second World War) there. Indeed, given the language division in this country, Toronto's hold on the life of Canada's West has no equal in the United States. This concentration of wealth and knowledge starves the rest of the country and contributes to the anti-metropolitan sentiments already mentioned.[34] One example of how this works is federal research policies and their effect on industry and universities. Increasingly these policies favour a "centres-of-excellence approach" which, given the disparity of local resources in Canada, cannot help but favour the centre over the periphery.

But there is no reason why Westerners should be only consumers of research, especially when much of it is the work of "expatriates." Because the federal government's contribution to research and development, while regrettably meagre by international standards, is nonetheless the major source of funds, this would appear a promising subject for federal-provincial negotiation. A change in policy, which saw research and development decentralized, would have long-term benefits for the areas of relocation. In view of the West's sudden but certainly transitory prosperity arising from energy sales, this is a field where hard bargaining could pay rich dividends.

Devolution differs from decentralization because it delegates authority to subordinate agents who thereby acquire the right to take initiatives. For a region isolated from political power at the centre, this is surely a most attractive feature. Decentralization limits choice by expanding government; devolution increases freedom by conferring power. Students of federalism might question the need to introduce devolution in a system where powers are already divided and institutions exist to make it work. The answer is that federalism does not work as far as the West is concerned. The integration once provided by political parties is gone. Cabinet government, as understood by all Canadian politicians save the Progressives, will not deviate from single-party rule (witness the N.D.P.'s abhorrence at even the suggestion of coalition in 1972). And parliament is not nor, given our political culture, can it be a congress. Yet the West must find some means of accommodating its interests in the federal system.

The traditional alternatives—Senate reform or a constitutional amendment to revise the division of powers—while reasonable in the abstract are politically impracticable. First, there must be an amending formula adopted, and then there must be agreement to change. Senate reform, which is perennially popular, never succeeds because any change that would actually convert it (even moderately) into a chamber of the provinces is critically studied by both federal and provincial governments who fear rivals. The advantages of devolution are that it is permissible constitutionally and benign legislatively (that is, power devolved or delegated is retrievable).

How then might it be used to the region's advantage? Two illustrations are the creation of a Western Canada Planning Council and a Western Canada Resources Development Council. These bodies would function as intermediaries between the provinces and the federal government where discussion, debate, and decisions could occur on subjects of immediate importance to the region.[35] Composed of individuals selected for a term by the provincial legislatures and parliament or perhaps with a proportion appointed by the provincial and federal governments, the councils would exercise powers conferred by the legislature and cabinet and, ideally, would provide the atmosphere for accommodation now lost to the anti-Liberal West. The conference of first ministers is staged on too grand a scale for true discussion. Instead, negotiations are conducted between semi-sovereign leaders who seek to influence each level's policies which are already formulated and maybe even announced.

Decentralization aims to give the region influence on federal policy as it is being formulated, while devolution seeks to provide control of policy when it is being implemented. This proposal recognizes the administrative revolution that has taken place in Canadian politics in the last fifty years. Where once "the culprits were the C.P.R. and the banks. Now, it is more likely to be the National Energy Board, the C.B.C., the Department of Transport (or any other choice of agencies) which appear as the decision-makers who ignore the aspiration of Western Canadians."[36] But the transformation has still broader implications for the political system. Regulatory bodies have been created in the main to deal with matters that require special knowledge or that are politically contentious. In each instance, it is believed that "parliament ought to ensure that politics is taken out of those decisions." The problem is that "any time there is a choice open to an administrator, [it] is by its essence a political choice."[37] Where the choice has definite regional implications, say the regulation of energy exports or the abandonment of rail lines, the potential for sectional conflict is increased.

To be sure, federal regulatory bodies, like all national committees, are constituted on a regional basis. But by virtue of its operation, this practice is no guarantee of equity. Moreover, the agencies' isolation from political supervision heightens the sense of impotence and injustice the region experiences when its interests are once again assumed to coincide with those of the nation. Whatever changes occur at the federal level, it would be desirable for the West to be able to assert some regional control, if only through the requirement that regulatory bodies report annually (documenting the reasons for their decision) to a body like the Planning Council referred to above.

The aim of these proposals is to reduce the suspicion of the federal government that currently thrives in Western Canada. This distrust has serious implications for the region and the nation, especially now that the economic terms of Confederation have shifted so strongly in favour of Alberta and, to a lesser extent, Saskatchewan. Governments, like individuals, fear uncertainty, and it was for this reason, as much as it was to protect mineral tax revenues, that the Saskatchewan government announced its plan in 1975 to nationalize the potash industry. Provincial governments cannot plan without some assurance that their predictions of the future are reasonably sound. The Blakeney government feared a repetition of Alberta's conflict with Ottawa. They judged that in the battle to control and develop the oil industry Alberta's government and people lost. There is no panacea for the region's dissent. The hoary grievance about freight rates is evidence of that.[38] These are only symptoms of the West's malaise. The problem goes much deeper because as the prime minister has perceptively noted: "There is a different culture in the West than there is in Central Canada. . . . It's not a different civilization but certainly it's a different form of culture than exists elsewhere."[39]

NOTES

1. To the list of political histories yet to be written should be added a comparative study of the West and Quebec in Confederation. For a reason, see Ramsay Cook, *Canada and the French-Canadian Question* (Toronto, 1966), pp. 95-96.
2. The Platforms are in Appendixes A, B, and C of W.L. Morton, *The Progressive Party in Canada* (Toronto, 1950), pp. 297-305.
3. Ibid., p. 298.
4. David E. Smith, *Prairie Liberalism: The Liberal Party in Saskatchewan* (Toronto, 1975), pp. 137-43.
5. John Stahl, "Prairie Agriculture: A Prognosis," in *Prairie Perspectives,* ed. David P. Gagan, (Toronto, 1970), pp. 58-76; Smith, *Prairie Liberalism, p.* 318.
6. Vernon C. Fowke, *The National Policy and the Wheat Economy* (Toronto, 1957), p. 71.
7. Ibid., p. 72.
8. P.C. 1589, 31 July 1919.
9. The campaign for the pool is described in *The Diary of Alexander James McPhail,* ed. Harold A. Innis (Toronto, 1940), chap. 2. See, too, H.S. Patton, *Grain Growers' Co-operation in Western Canada* (Cambridge, Mass., 1928).
10. Morton, *Progressive Party in Canada, p.* 156.
11. Canada, *Report of the Royal Commission on Dominion-Provincial Relations* (3 vols. in one, Ottawa, 1954), Vol. I, p. 150.
12. *Montreal Star,* 9 February 1956.
13. Statutes of Canada.
14. Norman Ward, "The Contemporary Scene," in *Politics in Saskatchewan,* ed. Norman Ward and Duff Spafford (Toronto, 1968), p. 287.
15. Province of Saskatchewan, "Opening Statement," Federal-Provincial Constitutional Conference, Ottawa, 10 February 1969, p. 1.
16. Saskatoon *Star-Phoenix,* 18 February 1970, p. 1.
17. Pierre E. Trudeau, "Social and Economic Objectives of the West," statement tabled at Western Economic Opportunities Conference by the

prime minister of Canada, 24 July 1973. See, also, the "Verbatim Record" of the three-day, Calgary meeting for an amplification of the prime minister's views as well as pertinent comments by the four western premiers.

18. Ibid.
19. C.B. Macpherson, *Democracy in Alberta: Social Credit and the Party System* (2nd ed., Toronto, 1962), p. 24.
20. Smith, *Prairie Liberalism,* p. 146.
21. See D.S. Spafford, " 'Independent' Politics in Saskatchewan before the Non-Partisan League," *Saskatchewan History* (Winter 1965), pp. 1-9; and Paul F. Sharp, *The Agrarian Revolt in Western Canada: A Study Showing American Parallels* (Minneapolis, 1948), chaps. 5 and 6.
22. The dilemmas of the Progressives are extensively chronicled in Morton's, *Progressive Party in Canada.*
23. Ibid., p. 292.
24. Fowke, *National Policy,* p. 200.
25. The best single explanation of the theory of group government is in Macpherson, *Democracy in Alberta,* chap. 2.
26. Walter Young, *The Anatomy of a Party: The National CCF, 1932-61* (Toronto, 1969), p. 15; Smith, *Prairie Liberalism,* p. 213.
27. W.L. Morton, "The Bias of Prairie Politics" in *Historical Essays on the Prairie Provinces,* ed. Donald Swainson (Toronto, 1970), p. 300.
28. For comments on the relative importance to policy of party caucus and cabinet, see Alan C. Cairns, "The Electoral System and the Party System in Canada, 1921-1965," *Canadian Journal of Political Science* (March 1968), pp. 55-80; and J.A.A. Lovink, "On Analysing the Impact of the Electoral System on the Party System in Canada," *Canadian Journal of Political Science* (Dec. 1970), pp. 497-516. See, too, J.A.A. Lovink, "Parliamentary Reform and Governmental Effectiveness in Canada," *Canadian Public Administration,* (Spring 1973), pp. 35-54.
29. Although made more than fifteen years ago by an Alberta Liberal, the following description of the party's decline is still accurate and is not limited to this province. "I tried to call a nominating convention and only five people came. At that meeting our president resigned as he is leaving town and there were not enough present to elect another president. . . . No candidate came forward. The feeling among the five present was that no person with any self-respect wants to run unless he is sure of winning. I have run and disagree." F. Olson to "Federation," 15 June 1959, National Liberal Federation Papers, P.A.C.
30. It is true that A.H. McDonald, leader from 1954 until 1959, only made it as a senator and W. Ross Thatcher was elected as a C.C.F. candidate in 1945 and sat as a socialist until 1956.
31. On the theory of elite accommodation, see *Consociational Democracy: Political Accommodation in Segmented Societies,* ed. Kenneth McRae (Toronto, 1974); and Robert Presthus, *Elite Accommodation in Canadian Politics* (Toronto, 1973). An unpublished paper that deals in passing with

elite accommodation and the West is Joseph Wearing, "Mutations in a Political Party: The Liberal Party of Canada in the Fifties and Sixties," prepared for the Annual Meeting of the Canadian Political Science Association, Edmonton, June 1975.

32. Otto Lang to Keith Davey (National Director), 29 September 1970, National Liberal Federation Papers, P.A.C.

33. Richard Simeon, *Federal-Provincial Diplomacy: The Making of Recent Policy in Canada* (Toronto, 1972).

34. Toronto is also the communications centre for English-speaking Canada.

35. Lloyd Axworthy, "Administrative Federalism and the West," paper presented to Liberal Conference on Western Objectives, Vancouver, July 1973.

36. Ibid., p. 5.

37. Canada, House of Commons, *Third Report of the Special Committee on Statutory Instruments, Session 1968-69* (Ottawa, 1969), p. 35. The speaker was the then minister of justice, John Turner.

38. Howard Darling, "What Belongs in Transportation Policy?" *Canadian Public Administration* (Winter 1975), pp. 665-66.

39. "Transcript of the Prime Minister's Speech at the Liberal Party Convention, Vancouver, July 15, 1973," p. 8 (in author's possession). Two pieces which explore the theme of regional culture are: Gerald Friesen, "The Western Canadian Identity," *CHR Historical Papers* (1973), pp. 13-19, and *A Region of the Mind: Interpreting the Western Canadian Plains,* ed. Richard Allen, (Regina, 1973).

COLIN D. HOWELL

Nova Scotia's Protest Tradition and the Search For a Meaningful Federalism*

Any analysis of Nova Scotia's protest tradition carries with it a temptation to exaggerate the province's cranky regionalism. It is important, therefore, to recognize that Nova Scotians have traditionally admitted the legitimacy of both local and national interests. While respect for local achievement tempers Nova Scotia's national allegiance, it is true as well that Nova Scotia's appreciation of the accomplishments of Confederation mitigates the acerbity of its provincial protest. Even in those periods when the province most ardently expressed its distrust of Confederation, its critique of Confederation went far beyond cantankerous parochialism. Indeed, an examination of three of Nova Scotia's more significant protest crusades—the Anti-Confederate movement of the 1860s, the repeal agitation of the 1880s, and the Maritime Rights agitation after the First World War—indicates the province's vulnerability to centralization and embodies a search for a more flexible and responsive federal system.[1]

* I am indebted throughout this paper to the advice and assistance of a number of colleagues. In particular, Robert Bollini, Burkhardt Kiesekamp, David Robson, and R.H. Cameron have offered extremely helpful suggestions and insights concerning the nature of the North American federalism.

Like any complex social phenomenon, the character of Nova Scotia's regional protest cannot be captured in a phrase. Boisterous, and at times bitter, Nova Scotian protest movements have been characterized by diversity. At various points they have attracted annexationists, Ontario-haters, advocates of independence, proponents of Maritime union, Imperialists, continentalists, and, ironically, even a few nationalists as well. The component parts of the movement, however, have formed a recognizable pattern. At the core of the movement was not merely a sense of frustration, but an essentially pragmatic political philosophy. The central conviction of Nova Scotian protest was that local interests were clearly as legitimate as any abstract notion of national right, and that the provincial legislature should defend those interests. But (and here is the rub), Confederation granted the provinces—the smaller ones in particular—no real defence against inequitable national policies initiated by the federal government. In cases where the central government is controlled by those who have little regard for provincial legislatures, or who consider local protest illegitimate, provinces suffering from what they consider unfair treatment are tempted—often against their better judgment—to raise the prospect of secession. When that happens it becomes even easier for the nationalist[2] to impeach local criticism as infantile, inflammatory, or intemperate, and to reproach local leaders for pandering to "irrational emotions" or "sectional prejudice."

At the time of her entry into Confederation, Nova Scotia's main concern was to avoid the sacrifice of local rights to the new national edifice. Despite Charles Tupper's conviction "that in a Union of British North America lay the only great future for any part of these provinces,"[3] there were many who saw Confederation as a menace. In particular, the decision of the provincial government to accept Confederation without putting the question to the electorate had created considerable unease. In the spring of 1866, a group of anti-Confederates established the League of Maritime Provinces and passed a series of resolutions opposing the union of Nova Scotia and the Canadas.[4] Even the passage of the B.N.A. Act itself could not stem the tide of opposition. In the elections of September 1867, anti-Confederates captured thirty-six of thirty-eight seats in the local legislature, and eighteen of nineteen seats in the Dominion parliament.

It is customary to link the anti-Confederate movement to the career of Joseph Howe. Howe, the father of responsible government in Nova Scotia, was an avid defender of Nova Scotian interests. Throughout his career he persistently urged London to accept the principle of consultation with the colonies in the formulation of Imperial policy. Any breach of that principle was likely to raise Howe's ire. It was Britain's failure to consult with Nova Scotia, for example, that occasioned both his opposition to the Reciprocity Treaty of 1854 and his subsequent demand for an Empire reorganized in such a way as to render the centre more responsive to local needs. Britain, he argued, "lost one-half of this continent by not comprehending it." It was thus important to make colonials "Britons in every sense of the word,"[5] by assuring consultation on issues that directly concerned them.

Despite his defence of Nova Scotia's local interests, Howe maintained an unflagging belief in the justice of the Imperial centre. Howe saw London as a repository of ethical government. The British parliament, he believed, contained an elevated order of schooled men who could appreciate interests other than their own, and hence could rise above their own selfishness. Yet, notwithstanding the talents of those who held Imperial office, the lack of any institutionalized procedure of consultation between the colonies and the Imperial centre rendered British institutions less effective than they should have been. Those in charge of colonial affairs at London, Howe wrote, "are men of genial manners, high attainments and varied information. . . . But what then? They have no personal knowledge of colonial public or social life; no hold upon the confidence and affections of the outlying portions of the Empire."[6] London's incomplete understanding of colonial realities prompted Howe to demand colonial representation in the Imperial parliament. Not only would this provide the opportunity for the locality to defend its interests at London, but it would enroll colonials in the "highest school of politics for the better discharge of their duties at home."[7]

Howe's faith in the competence of the Imperial centre explains his reluctance to support Canadian Confederation and his concomitant antipathy towards the idea of autonomous local legislatures. Because a Canadian nation could never provide the impartial and judicious government characteristic of London, Confederation would result in the triumph of the strongest interest. The larger provinces would quickly come to dominate the smaller ones. At the same time, Howe opposed the principle of subordinate jurisdictions sharing power with a central parliament. "England tried to work an Imperial Parliament in harmony with local legislatures," he wrote in January 1865, "found the system impracticable, and swept them... away. Why shall we try over again an experiment which the experience of the Mother Country condemns?"[8] What Howe wanted was the continuance of Imperial stewardship. Failing that, he would prefer a unitary state unencumbered by those divisive local jurisdictions likely to weaken national authority: "Before a single step is taken to disturb the existing order of things, let us know what we are to have instead. If we are to be colonies, then let us put on no airs, and create no divided allegiance or authority. If we are to be a nation, then let us set about the serious work we are assuming with a full sense of its perilous obligations."[9]

Howe opposed Confederation, not because it gave too much power to the central legislature,[10] but because representation by population would provide the smaller provinces no real defence against inequitable policies initiated by the Canadian parliament. "In our case we have a confederacy in name," he wrote, "but in reality the centre of power will always be in Canada." Howe also believed that the provincial legislature would provide no defence of local interests. In the new union, Howe concluded, Nova Scotia would be "as powerless as Hanover or Brunswick in the grasp of Bismarck."[11] His answer to this problem was to vest the substantial power of government in an elected Senate with equal representation for the provinces. This would create a political centre free from domination by selfish interests, and render the idea of cooperative federalism and shared power unnecessary.

In February 1868, the province of Nova Scotia dispatched Howe, William Annand, Jared C. Troop, and J. W. Smith to

London to make the case for independence one final time. If Howe had any hope that repeal was possible before his trip to London, he had none when he returned. The British Colonial Office, through the Duke of Buckingham, made it clear that Nova Scotian independence was impossible. For one thing, New Brunswick had entered the union assuming that Nova Scotia would join as well. Buckingham argued that "vast obligations, political and commercial, have already been contracted,"[12] and could not be overturned. This was something of an exaggeration, but did make clear London's determined opposition to repeal.

Once Howe was convinced that independence was a dead issue, he began to entertain the prospects of a bargain with Sir John A. Macdonald's Conservative government at Ottawa. Given Howe's faith in strong central government, his attraction to Macdonald is understandable. Like Howe, Macdonald was a centrist who had little respect for provincial legislatures. Both men, too, feared the eventual absorption of Canada by the United States, and staunchly defended the superiority of British institutions over their republican counterparts. The result of Howe's bargain with Macdonald—besides Howe's inclusion in the Conservative cabinet—was a readjustment of the financial terms of Confederation. Under the new arrangement, Nova Scotia received an annual subsidy of $82,698 per annum, and an increase in the provincial debt allowance from $8,000,000 to $9,186,000.[13]

Despite Howe's defection from the repeal campaign, the provincial government continued to fight against Confederation. Men like William Annand and Attorney-General Martin Wilkins—although they considered independence an unlikely prospect—continued to oppose union because they saw the national edifice as a threat rather than a boon to local autonomy. They were also convinced that the provincial legislature provided the only real check against excessive centralization. Of the two, Wilkins was the more uncompromising. Wilkins argued that the B.N.A. Act was unconstitutional because it exceeded the competence of parliament to alter the character of the Empire without gaining the consent of the affected colonies,[14] and advocated that the province raise a tariff against the Canadians to demonstrate its independence. In addition, he suggested that if Nova Scotians were "not strong enough to resist the Canadians, and were determined to free themselves by force, they could obtain the aid of other nations."[15]

In retrospect, the localism of men like Wilkins and Annand—uncompromising though it might have been—was a necessary component of Nova Scotia's first "provincial rights" movement. Annand and Wilkins were not crackpots or woolyheaded extremists by any means. Instead, they were localists who were convinced that the nationalist bias of the Macdonald government had created a central authority not only unsympathetic, but threatening, to local autonomy. At the same time, after the London mission of 1868, neither was so naive as to contemplate secession as a real possibility. Thereafter, the repeal agitation was less an attempt to secure independence than an effort to shape the character of the new union; it involved an attempt to assert Canada's federal character in the face of those who would define it as a unitary nation state.

The change of government at Ottawa in November 1873, and the ascent to power of the Liberals, did much to encourage the national allegiance of earlier anti-Confederates. The lure of office attached former anti-Confederates to the national government, but, more important, the Reform administration of Alexander Mackenzie entertained little of Macdonald's disdain for provincial jurisdictions. Consequently, attachment to the centre seemed less perilous than before. Annand's Halifax *Morning Chronicle*, formerly an avid exponent of repeal, believed it time "to deal with the live issues of the present, not the dead issue of the past."[16] In place of repeal, the *Chronicle* editorialized in favour of the federalist notion that both local and national intentions had a concurrent legitimacy: "If the Dominion is to prosper, as we all hope and expect it will, all rivalries and jealousies between the different Provinces must cease, and the people of all sections be united in a determination not only to have their local and personal interests advanced, but to have the government carried on in such a manner as will promote the good of the country."[17] By 1873, then, the earlier localism of the anti-Confederate movement had evolved into an acceptance of Canada as a federal state.

A decade later, a renewed wave of protest feeling swept the province. In May 1886, acting in response to the acute financial disabilities of the Nova Scotian government, Premier Fielding's Liberal party introduced and sustained a series of repeal resolutions in the provincial legislature. In the ensuing election of 15 June, the Liberals won a striking victory; twenty-nine of the province's thirty-eight seats fell to Fielding. This second repeal movement indicated the province's disenchantment with a renewed nationalism at Ottawa, occasioned by the return to power of Macdonald and the Conservatives in 1878. Contemptuous of local authority, Macdonald had once written "that the General Government or Parliament should pay no more regard to the status or position of the Local Governments than it would to the prospects of the ruling party in the corporation of Quebec or Montreal."[18] During the 1880s, Macdonald refused to stray from this nationalist orthodoxy. With the emergence of a number of "provincial rights" campaigns in the 1880s, Macdonald became convinced that any demonstration of weakness by the centre would threaten national unity. Macdonald thus refused to yield to Nova Scotia's demands; between 1879 and 1886 he repeatedly refused to act upon requests from the provincial government for assistance in meeting its deepening financial crisis.[19]

Throughout this period, the province attempted to establish a reasonable settlement of its financial difficulties, but got little help from Macdonald. As early as 1878, in the wake of the discontinuance of Joseph Howe's "better terms" annuity of 1869, the Holmes-Thompson administration made an initial representation to Ottawa for a subsidy increase, pointing out the very real financial crisis facing the province. The reply was a stinging rebuke. The deputy minister of finance, in a patronizing fashion, suggested that "if the public moneys were husbanded with greater frugality ... an equilibrium might be established between receipts and expenditures."[20] Ottawa's suggestions of economy, however, made it no easier for the province to govern itself. Any unexpected expenditure, such as the expense of repairing a number of large bridges damaged during the heavy spring freshets of 1883,[21] exerted a strain on provincial finances that affected other necessities, or added to the provincial debt.[22]

During the 1880s, requests for "better terms" came from both sides of the House. In 1884, for example, the Conservatives joined with Fielding's government in demanding relief. In a memorial to the governor general, the province argued "that an additional revenue has become an absolute necessity to this Province . . . as our people will not submit to direct taxation for local purposes."[23] The federal government did not reply. By this time, some members of the legislature, led by James A. Fraser of Guysborough, began to demand a sterner course of action, and pressed Fielding to take up repeal. But Fielding was not to be stampeded. Late in 1884 he persuaded Fraser to hold his fire momentarily in order that Edward Blake might raise the "better terms" question in the House of Commons.[24] In turn, Fielding wrote to Blake suggesting that the matter be brought up in Parliament by a Nova Scotian M.P.—perhaps by Mr. Kirk from Guysborough—on a motion for correspondence. Once that was done, Fielding suggested, Blake should indicate his sympathy for Nova Scotia's plight and argue in favour of a readjustment of Nova Scotia's subsidy. Without a discussion of the issue in parliament, Fielding warned, "men who have hesitated to commit themselves to a repeal cry will no longer hesitate" to do so.[25]

But the character of the federal Liberal party inhibited a favourable response to Nova Scotia's difficulties. Blake was embarrassed by the issue. Ontario's Liberals, despite their antipathy to Macdonald's nationalism, had little interest in Nova Scotia's financial problems. If anything they opposed "better terms" on the grounds that Ontario would assume the cost of any new financial arrangement. Despite Fielding's urgings, therefore, Blake was in no position to address Nova Scotia's plight.

By the summer of 1885, Fielding had exhausted all the available options short of repeal, and nothing had yet been done to relieve the province's difficulties. In desperation, Fielding dispatched a final letter to Macdonald in July 1885, reiterating "the absolute necessity of larger grants . . . for the support of services assigned the Local Government."[26] Fielding further advised that if no relief was forthcoming, he would contemplate removing Nova Scotia from Confederation. Despite this naked threat of repeal, it was a full six months before the province heard back from Ottawa. It was hardly worth the wait. Macdonald rejected the province's request, pointing out curtly that Nova Scotia had "withdrawn from the credit of the debt account large amounts which they had expended on Railway extension."[27]

While there was some truth to Macdonald's remarks, most Nova Scotians considered his abrupt and dilatory reply a further indication of Ottawa's indifference to Nova Scotia's financial impoverishment. The *Morning Chronicle* was irate: "That announcement calls for a most important change of some sort in Nova Scotian politics. The province cannot live upon its present income. . . . Only two alternatives are open to us—direct taxation or repeal."[28] The *Chronicle's* remarks went to the heart of the matter. Expenditures necessary to maintain the services required of the provincial government increased annually, while the major part of provincial revenues remained unchanged.[29] Direct taxation was a possible solution, but any government that moved to institute it was unlikely to survive. As Fielding pointed out, there could be no stronger indictment of Confederation in Nova Scotia than the initiation of direct taxation. "If we must now resort to direct taxation . . . then the case for repeal is complete," Fielding wrote. "Direct taxation was held up by the anti-Confederates as one of the probable results of the Union. The Government that resorts to such a tax . . . will be quickly swept away."[30]

Fielding believed that much of the problem facing the province had its roots in the Confederation settlement. Because the agreement of 1867 had not placed substantial revenue sources at the disposal of the provinces, the solution of provincial difficulties often depended upon the largesse of the centre.[31] Confederation had created a legislative union in the guise of a federal state: the B.N.A. Act had placed the preponderance of power in the hands of the federal government. Accordingly, whenever the centre was captured by those who had little concern for local governments, the community faced an increase in sectional tension and an erosion of national consensus. As a result, Fielding stressed the need for a more responsive federalism. He wrote: "I am strongly opposed to the idea of a Legislative Union. If we are to remain united I believe Nova Scotia should have a Local Legislature and Government with sufficient power and means to command respect."[32]

Just how far the province was willing to go in its repudiation of the Macdonaldian vision of Confederation became apparent on 5 May 1886, when Fielding's government passed a resolution favouring repeal of the British North America Act. But the resolution itself was misleading; Fielding had no desire to disrupt Confederation. What he wanted was "better terms." In his election manifesto of 18 May 1886, he pointed out that as soon as the provincial government initiated its repeal resolutions, the federal government offered to extend the Intercolonial Railway from the Strait of Canso to Louisbourg. "If that was the immediate result of just shaking a repeal resolution at them," said Fielding, "what might be expected when the people of Nova Scotia endorsed the resolution at the polls."[33]

If Fielding expected his followers in the Liberal party to support him in his repeal campaign, he was disappointed. While most Nova Scotians eschewed the idea of a highly centralized nation-state, very few of them wished to see the disruption of Confederation. To support a repeal resolution in the legislature was one thing—it could be explained as a gentlemanly protest against Macdonald's recalcitrance—but to support repeal on the hustings was altogether different. Indeed, with the exception of James A. Fraser and Otto Weeks in Guysborough, W. F. McCoy in Shelburne, William Law in Yarmouth, and Jeffrey McColl in Pictou, most Liberal candidates and influential party organizers avoided the issue throughout the campaign. William Pipes, Fielding's predecessor as premier, was so incensed that he publicly berated the government for dragging out "the putrid carcass of repeal."[34] Similarly, J. W. Carmichael, the New Glasgow merchant and former anti-Confederate, was "disappointed and disgusted with our local Gov'ts [sic] course on repeal."[35] It made more sense, Carmichael believed, to demand a "remodelling of our constitution ... and an absolute defined settlement of the relations of the province to the Federal Government."[36]

A number of Liberal newspapers also shrank from advocating repeal. While William Annand of the Halifax *Morning Chronicle* was again calling for freedom from the "exactions of Canucks,"[37] New Glasgow's S. M. McKenzie, editor of the Liberal *Eastern Chronicle* kicked off his campaign with the following disclaimer: "Our taxes have been largely increased, and we have seen them squandered in the wildnesses of British Columbia and in the slaughter of our fellow-countrymen in the North-West, yet our local services have been absolutely starved during all these years. . . . While all this . . . affords great excuse for the measures adopted by Mr. Fielding and his followers, we cannot follow him to the full extent of his resolutions."[38] Other newspapers were also reluctant to support Fielding. In Halifax, the *Acadian Recorder* hardly mentioned repeal, arguing instead for reciprocity with the United States. Elsewhere, the Liverpool *Advance* and the Truro *Guardian* chose to ignore the issue completely, while in Cape Breton not a voice was raised in its support.

Fielding thus faced an array of problems. In the first place, as Charles Hibbert Tupper remarked, the Liberals became "a party united solely by party ties but divided on this question of repeal."[39] Secondly, when the electorate gave Fielding's government a hearty endorsement on 15 June, the Liberals found it virtually impossible to decide what the election results meant. Did they represent a vote of confidence in Fielding's effective administration, or were they a mandate for carrying the secession campaign into the forthcoming federal election contest?

In Halifax, Fielding and Alfred G. Jones saw no alternative but to carry on with repeal. J. W. Carmichael demurred. To continue to talk secession, he remonstrated, would be a "terrible blunder"[40] likely to lead the Liberal party to ruin. Carmichael questioned the judgment of both Fielding and Jones: "When the policy was announced . . . the main idea was, that it should be used as a lever to obtain better terms, but the overwhelming victory fairly dazed the Gov't.[*sic*] and our friends in Halifax. They are miscalculating the real value of the repeal movement."[41] Despite Carmichael's caveat, it was asking too much for the Liberal party to shelve the issue. At the very least it might yet prompt a "better terms" arrangement. Furthermore, to ignore repeal during the federal campaign would impugn the sincerity of those who had endorsed repeal during the provincial election of 1886. Out and out separatists would criticize the party for its unwillingness to act upon the apparent repeal mandate. To emphasize secession, on the other hand, was equally dangerous. A strong repeal campaign would drive more moderate Liberals into Macdonald's arms. The party's answer to this dilemma—and not a very effective one at that—was to waffle. In the subsequent federal campaign, the Liberals neither emphasized nor repudiated repeal.[42]

In the federal election of 1887, the repeal issue became the Liberal party's albatross. In part this stemmed from the fact that the provincial party—despite its repeal advocacy—was an adjunct of the national Liberal party. During the campaign, Liberal candidates found themselves in the uncomfortable position of supporting Edward Blake as national party leader while tolerating the apparently destructive policy of secession. This contradiction was embarrassing and ultimately fatal. The Conservative Antigonish *Casket* pointed out that if the Liberals "are earnest Repealers they are not supporters of Blake, if they are supporters of Blake, they are not earnest Repealers."[43] The Halifax *Morning Herald* was even more cryptic: "Whatever his other weaknesses," it suggested, ". . . Blake is not yet a secessionist."[44]

Repeal was not the only difficulty. The position of Liberal candidates in the province was further eroded by Blake's equivocating stand on the tariff. In speeches at Malvern, Simcoe, and East York, Ontario, Blake all but admitted the impossibility of a major downward revision of the tariff.[45] In so doing he weakened the hands of those Liberal candidates in Nova Scotia who were campaigning on the baleful effects of the National Policy. The *Morning Herald* gloated: "It is extremely amusing, as we have frequently pointed out, to find the *Chronicle* constantly abusing the national policy, while the Grit leaders of the upper provinces are soothing their protectionist friends with the song of the siren that 'the tariff is not in danger.' "[46] Taken together, the equivocation concerning both the repeal issue and the National Policy resulted in the Liberal party's undoing.

Macdonald's Conservatives won fourteen of twenty-one Nova Scotia seats in the election of 1887. The difficulties Nova Scotia Liberals experienced in 1887 indicate the extent to which national party organizations are unable to accommodate themselves to the language of local discontent. In 1886, in the context of provincial politics, repeal had made eminently good sense: it offered voters a chance to register their disapproval of Macdonald's disregard for the province's financial plight. But, in the broader context of federal politics, it was difficult to mount an effective repeal agitation. In 1887, national party considerations tended to conflict with and override those of the province, and thus assured the demise of the secession crusade. This points to an enduring difficulty in our federal system. In effect, the smaller provinces are powerless to defend themselves against cavalier use of federal power. Although Ottawa's disregard for legitimate local needs frequently occasions a "provincial rights" agitation, our federal parties are structured in such a way that regional grievances can often be ignored with impunity. In the long run, however, this carries a heavy price. Each time the federal government blithely ignores provincial interests or cavalierly asserts its national prerogative it devitalizes the union and undermines national consensus.

The difficulty inherent in using the provincial wing of a national party to promote regional protest was less apparent in Nova Scotia's postwar Maritime Rights crusade than it had been earlier. But it was evident nevertheless. As was true of the repeal agitation of the 1880s, Nova Scotia's postwar protest was intimately linked to partisan politics. With Mackenzie King's Liberal government in power at Ottawa, E. H. Armstrong's provincial Liberal government was unwilling to attack Ottawa for its failure to address Nova Scotia's deepening postwar recession. As a result the provincial Conservative party—an adjunct of that party at Ottawa which was traditionally committed to political centralization—came to absorb the Maritime Rights protest of the early 1920s in the hope of dislodging the Liberals from power. It was a successful tactic. In the provincial election of 1925 the Conservative party under E. N. Rhodes humiliated the Armstrong government, winning forty of the province's forty-three seats.[47]

The Maritime Rights movement fed upon the idea that the policies of the central authority abridged local initiative and hampered local development. It gained widespread support. W. H. Dennis, owner of the Halifax *Herald* and the Halifax *Mail*, H. S. Congdon, editor of the Dartmouth *Patriot*, A. M. Belding, editor of the Saint John *Telegraph*, Robert Hattie, editor of the *Maritime Merchant*, and the aging James A. Fraser, editor of the New Glasgow *Eastern Chronicle*, all gave the campaign their active editorial endorsement. The Maritime Boards of Trade vigorously promoted the campaign as well. The basic strategy of the movement was to demand Nova Scotia's rights rather than to seek "handouts" from Ottawa. Proponents of Maritime Rights thus rejected the description of the Maritimes as an unfortunate poor relation always grumbling and supplicating the other members of the family for assistance. "This sort of thing," the *Maritime Merchant* observed, "is fearfully irritating to a proud people, particularly when they know that they have made sacrifices for those who regard them as mendicants."[48]

The basic argument made by proponents of Maritime Rights was that inequitable national policies had undermined the promise of Confederation in Nova Scotia. The protective tariff graphically illustrated the way in which local interests had been sacrificed upon the altar of national authority. In a speech to the Canadian Club in 1925, F. B. McCurdy pointed out that the tariff attracted foreign capital and built up the industrial base of Central Canada at the expense of outlying areas. Of 1,500 branch plants established after 1900, he observed, not one had been established in Nova Scotia.[49] Robert Hattie echoed these sentiments in the editorial columns of the *Maritime Merchant*. "It has not escaped the notice of people in the maritime provinces," he wrote, "that this development has occurred to the benefit chiefly of the provinces of Ontario and Quebec."[50] It was Hattie's belief that the national policy was so prejudicial to Nova Scotian business development that there was no real incentive for American branch plants to locate in the province. And, because the tariff stimulated regional disparity, it was ludicrous to describe it as a truly "national" policy.

The freight-rate question, which is discussed in detail by Ernest Forbes above, provided another example of Nova Scotia's vulnerability to decisions made outside the region. Because of the heavy losses incurred by the Intercolonial Railway, the rates on east and westbound shipments were equalized in May 1912. For the Maritimes, the result was a cumulative rate increase of approximately 92 per cent, almost twice the estimated average increase for the rest of Canada.[51] With the absorption of the Intercolonial into the Canadian National system, a new Railway Traffic Board in Montreal issued rates on local traffic. The result was an inevitable tendency towards the rationalization of freight rates, with little heed paid to varying regional needs and conditions. Fearful of alienating local shippers in other parts of Canada, the board refrained from approving low rates for local traffic in the Maritimes.[52]

The Railway Traffic Board's assumption that a mile is a mile wherever you find it, had a disastrous effect upon Nova Scotia's economic life. The rationalization of freight rates coupled with the economic dislocation surrounding postwar demobilization occasioned a serious economic recession. Shipping declined, business failures increased, wholesale warehousers lost their customers, and the province experienced a considerable exodus of skilled workers and professional men.[53] Cape Breton was particularly hard hit. The basic problem here was the shrinking market for Cape Breton coal, which had led the recently formed British Empire Steel Corporation to cut wages by more than a third in January 1922. For the next few years Cape Breton was in a turmoil; and, to make matters worse, Mackenzie King's Liberal government did little to address the painful economic conditions that the miners faced.[54]

The accumulated troubles facing the province in the early twenties resulted in a resurgence of separatist feeling. In New Glasgow, James A. Fraser, the leading advocate of repeal during the 1880s, continued to call for Nova Scotia's withdrawal from Confederation. Repeal sentiment, moreover, tended to grow in proportion to King's apparent disregard for Nova Scotia's plight. George Wilson of Dalhousie University commented upon the remarkable growth of anti-Confederate sentiment in Nova Scotia in 1924 and 1925. "A year ago," he wrote in March 1925, "I was at a Liberal convention met to nominate a candidate to contest . . . a by-election. The proposer of the successful candidate, amidst great applause, said he voted against Confederation in 1867 and that if he had the opportunity, he would vote the same way tomorrow."[55] In a similar vein, W. H. Dennis warned Arthur Meighen that unless effective leadership was promoted in the province, "desperate men with desperate methods who care nothing for a united Canada, are willing to lead a secession movement for their own selfish interests."[56]

But the Maritime Rights movement never blossomed into a full-blown repeal crusade. For one thing, the intimate connection between the provincial and national Conservatives limited independent action at the local level. In April 1923, H. W. Corning, Conservative leader in the Nova Scotia legislature, presented a resolution arguing that the spirit of the Confederation settlement had been violated. Nova Scotia, he argued, was handicapped by high freight rates, a high protective tariff, underdevelopment of Atlantic ports, and a heavy burden of taxation. Corning proceeded to demand a referendum on the question of secession from Canada and the establishment of Nova Scotia as an independent community within the British Empire.[57] But the party quickly dispensed with the repeal issue. The Conservatives chose only to outline the economic injustice under which the province laboured and to demand redress. Instead of advocating repeal, the Conservative party platform of 1925 argued that it would be necessary to approach the British government for an amendment of the B.N.A. Act if provincial demands concerning freight rates and trade adjustments were not met.[58]

It was evident in the provincial submission to the Duncan Royal Commission on Maritime Claims in 1926 that the leaders of the Maritime Rights movement could never escape their loyalty to the national Conservative party, despite their local sensibilities. The author of the Nova Scotia submission, Colonel E. C. Phinney, was president of the Liberal-Conservative Association in Nova Scotia. Particularly concerned that the promise of Confederation had not been realized in Nova Scotia, Phinney had once confided to a friend that "if some relief from tariff burdens were not secured, he would go as far as to agitate secession from Confederation."[59] But Phinney's later brief demonstrated little of that belligerence; instead it tended to let national party interests take precedence over local problems. Although Phinney's brief dealt with both the freight-rate question and the inflexible financial arrangements between Ottawa and the provinces, it virtually ignored the effect of the tariff upon Nova Scotia's development. Phinney's explanation was that the Tariff Advisory Board was already investigating tariff schedules on coal, iron, and steel. A more likely reason was that a full discussion of the issue would embarrass the national party which was currently attacking King for his low-tariff orientation.[60]

The Report of the Duncan Commission concluded that Nova Scotia had indeed suffered within Confederation. It advocated a 20-per-cent freight-rate reduction on all traffic which both originated and terminated in stations of the Atlantic Division and destined outside the region. In 1927, Mackenzie King accepted the recommendations of the Duncan Commission and within a year of the Commission Report the rate reductions had become law.[61] The Duncan Commission had not, however, examined the effect of the tariff upon Nova Scotia's development. It was left to Norman McLeod Rogers, a Nova Scotia political scientist and eventual Liberal cabinet minister in Mackenzie King's government, to clarify the province's position on this question. In a brief to the 1934 Jones Commission on Nova Scotia's welfare within Confederation, Rogers outlined the prejudicial impact that tariff and transportation policies exerted upon the economic life of Nova Scotia. The tariff, he pointed out, was a tax upon Nova Scotians and a subsidy for the central provinces.[62] Using 1931 as his year of computation, Rogers concluded that the tariff operated as a duty of $12.28 per capita in Nova Scotia, and as a subsidy of $11.03 and $15.15 per capita respectively in Quebec and Ontario.[63] Furthermore, in encouraging industry to locate in Central Canada rather than in Nova Scotia, the tariff operated to reduce the tax base, thus rendering the province less able to provide necessary social services.

By the mid-thirties, however, the tariff was not the only problem facing Nova Scotia. The worsening depression had also revealed the unusually rigid character of the financial terms of Confederation. Neither the financial settlement of 1867, which provided for an annual grant of 80 cents per head and an additional sum of $60,000 in support of the government and Legislature, nor the revision of 1907 which increased the latter subsidy by more than $120,000, had provided the province with enough revenue to meet the depression crisis.[64] To Rogers, this demonstrated the need for frequent readjustments of dominion-provincial subsidy arrangements. He wrote: "Stability for a fixed term may be possible of achievement, but to seek to stabilize provincial subsidies in perpetuity was both impolitic and impossible. . . . The financial relations of federalism are influenced by the rapid currents and cross-currents of economic change. Ease of conscious adjustment is more important than stability in the financial relations of any federal state." What was needed, Rogers believed, was a revision of the British North America Act in order to ensure easier adjustment of the financial relations of the Dominion and the provinces.[65]

Rogers was the ultimate federalist. Convinced that Canada's diversity demanded a recognition of the legitimacy of competing interests or multiple allegiances, Rogers championed a pragmatic, brokerage style of politics. Above all else, he believed, the fundamental task of political life was to keep the community together. In a regionally diverse nation like Canada, however, it was inevitable that differences would emerge. Rogers therefore called for a federal system flexible enough to handle these differences expeditiously. The prerequisite for this more meaningful federalism was a recognition of the concurrent legitimacy of local and national intentions. "If we recognize . . . sectional claims and differences as normal incidents in our growth," Rogers wrote, "we are more likely to approach them in a spirit which will not weaken the essential foundation of our national life."[66]

Throughout its history, Nova Scotia has experienced great difficulty in fulfilling its local objectives, and in shaping national policies to its own advantage. For the most part, Joseph Howe's prediction of a century ago that smaller provinces like Nova Scotia would be overwhelmed in Confederation has been borne out. Although Nova Scotia's provincial governments have been successful in wringing some minor concessions from Ottawa, they have not been successful in assuring equitable advantage for the province within Confederation. A recognition of the legitimacy of Nova Scotia's local intentions would help address her difficulties, but this alone will not solve the serious problems of regional disparity that confront the area.

Given the historical inability of the provincial government to protect Nova Scotia against unfair national policies, what might be done to create a more equitable federal system? One possibility is to take up Joseph Howe's suggestion that the character and function of the Canadian Senate be altered and expanded to provide a more effective defence of provincial interests. An elected Senate with equal provincial representation would provide the kind of protection against inequitable national policies that the provincial legislature has been unable to provide. Senate reform can take a number of forms. Each province, for example, might be granted six senators each serving a six-year term, and two of whom would stand for re-election every second year. By rotating the senatorial elections, moreover, the opportunity would arise to introduce a system of senatorial primaries which would subordinate national party allegiance to local concerns.

Failing a widespread reform of the Senate, the provinces could express their opinion on federal appointments to the Senate through a provincial initiative and referendum. Unfortunately, there is an assumption—as common as it is misguided—that the initiative and referendum are not working devices. While these proposals were endorsed by the Progressives and the United Farmers movements in the 1920s, they have never been written into the statute books of any province. But the initiative and referendum can represent an effective lever for the provincial jurisdiction. In the western United States, for example, state administrations employ these devices both to marshal local consensus in support of provincial innovations and to shape and articulate provincial resistance to the central authority. They have been of particular value in questions of land reclamation, water purification, power development, and resource allocation. Furthermore, because the introduction of "direct democracy" would make the provincial political apparatus more accessible to the public, it would counteract the widespread political defeatism in the smaller provinces that has made a vital provincial political life virtually impossible.

Ultimately, however, serious institutional reforms are only

possible if Canadians come to realize that loyalty to the national community derives not from enforced sacrifice, but from local and personal satisfaction. As members of a regionally diverse community, we must avoid the temptation to regard local objectives as ethically flawed or "selfish" merely because they are local. This message was central to the Nova Scotian protest tradition. Behind each outburst of Nova Scotian protest rests the complaint that existing national policies threaten legitimate local enterprise. And, as the recent controversy over freight-rate increases in Nova Scotia indicates, Nova Scotia's vulnerability to decisions made without regard for regional variation undermines the province's national allegiance.

If Canadians hope to secure a more cohesive community in the 1970s and 1980s, it will be important to recognize the legitimacy of our regional and local allegiances. But how can we encourage this recognition? One possibility is to introduce a widespread program of citizenship education, including the expansion and development of regional studies programs and student exchange arrangements in our schools and universities. In addition, such a program should be made available to members of our federal bureaucracy and the national media; in short, to those most responsible for formulating national policy and shaping public opinion. Obviously, Canada's national policies—whether they involve transportation policy, resource development, or limitations on foreign capital investment—must take into account the varying needs of different regions and provinces. If they do not, the meaning of Confederation will be brought into question. Confederation will defeat its primary purpose if its national policies continue to encourage the gradual debilitation of the smaller provinces rather than addressing the challenge of regional disparity. A more flexible federal system will help Canada meet that challenge.

NOTES

1. See Robert Bollini, "Confederate Politics and the National Wisdom," unpublished paper, Halifax Conference on Ethics and Public Policy, Halifax, August 1974.
2. Throughout this paper I have availed myself of the lexicon of nationalism

worked out in the European context. In European parlance, it is traditional to define a nation-state as a highly centralized community distrustful of subordinate legislative autonomy. In this regard, see Leonard F. Krieger, "Nationalism and the Nation-State System," in *Chapters in Western Civilization*, ed. Joseph Blau, Ralph Bowen et al., 2 vols. (3rd edition, New York, 1962), Vol. II, pp. 103-39; and *The German Idea of Freedom* (Boston, 1957). Also useful is the recent *Royal Commission on the Constitution, 1969-1973*, 2 vols. (London, 1973), and in particular, Lord Crowther Hunt and Professor A.T. Peacock, "Memorandum of Dissent," Vol. II, chap. II, section 34, p. 11, where the point was made that the United Kingdom is the largest and most centralized unitary state in western Europe. This definition of the nation-state is at variance with that offered by Ramsay Cook in his stimulating and thought-provoking essay, "Nationalism and the Nation-State," in his *The Maple Leaf Forever: Essays on Nationalism and Politics in Canada* (Toronto, 1971), pp. 1-22. Cook describes the nation-state as a functional unit which "serves the practical purpose of organizing groups of people into manageable units and providing them with services which they need and can share" (p. 8).

3. *The Life and Letters of the Right Hon. Sir Charles Tupper, Bart., K.C.M.G.,* 2 vols., ed. E.M. Saunders (Toronto, 1916), Vol. I, p. 147.

4. R.H. Campbell, "The Repeal Agitation in Nova Scotia, 1867-1869," Nova Scotia Historical Society, *Collections,* Vol. XXV (1942), p. 99.

5. J.A. Chisholm, *The Speeches and Public Letters of Joseph Howe,* 2 vols. (Halifax, 1909), Vol. II, p. 277.

6. Ibid., II, p. 292.

7. Ibid., II, p. 498.

8. Botheration Letter No. 2, *Morning Chronicle,* 13 January 1865; also quoted in J. Murray Beck, *Joseph Howe: The Voice of Nova Scotia* (Toronto, 1964), p. 173. Howe was referring here to the Parliaments of Scotland and Ireland that were legislated out of existence in 1707 and 1801 respectively.

9. Chisholm, *Speeches,* II, p. 488.

10. P.B. Waite, *The Life and Times of Confederation 1864-1867: Politics, Newspapers, and the Union of British North America* (Toronto, 1962), pp. 193-228. Waite argues that much of the opposition to Confederation in Halifax emanated from a belief that the central authority in the new confederacy would not be strong enough to act decisively. Howe echoed these sentiments.

11. Chisholm, *Speeches,* II, pp. 490-91.

12. Duke of Buckingham to Lord Monck, 4 June 1868, Nova Scotia, *Journals of the House of Assembly,* 1868, No. 10, pp. 49-51; (hereafter referred to as *Journals.)*

13. J.A. Maxwell, *Federal Subsidies to Provincial Governments in Canada* (Cambridge, Mass., 1937), p. 28.

14. Kenneth George Pryke, "Nova Scotia and Confederation 1864-1870" (PH. D. thesis, Duke University, 1962), pp. 178-79.

15. Nova Scotia, *Debates,* 3 September 1868; reported in *Morning Chronicle,* 4 September 1868.

16. *Morning Chronicle,* 10 January 1874.

17. Ibid., 31 December 1873.
18. G.V. LaForest, *Disallowance and Reservation of Provincial Legislation* (Ottawa, 1955), p. 53.
19. Colin D. Howell, "Repeal, Reciprocity, and Commercial Union in Nova Scotia Politics, 1886-1887" (MA thesis, Dalhousie University, 1967), pp. 10-14.
20. *Journals,* 1882, Appendix No. 14, p. 49, quoted in J. Murray Beck, *The Government of Nova Scotia* (Toronto, 1957), p. 329.
21. Nova Scotia, *Debates,* 25 February 1886.
22. Any suggestion of financial irresponsibility on the part of the province was clearly unwarranted. Fielding, in a letter to Edward Blake, pointed out that only one member of the provincial civil service received a salary in excess of $3,000, one received $2,000, and all the rest $1,600 and below. There were, moreover, only three salaried portfolios in the government, the united salaries amounting only to $6,000. At the same time, so severe were Nova Scotia's financial problems that the province could neither afford to replace a defective heating system at Province House, nor repair the sidewalks around the building. Fielding to Blake, 8 January 1886, Nos. 157-58, Fielding Papers, Public Archives of Nova Scotia (hereafter P.A.N.S.).
23. *Journals,* 1886, Appendix No. 12, p. 5.
24. Fielding to Blake, 15 July 1885, No. 654, Fielding Papers.
25. Fielding to Blake, 6 July 1885, No. 634, Fielding Papers.
26. *Journals,* 1886, Appendix No. 12, p. 6.
27. Ibid., p. 13.
28. *Morning Chronicle,* 26 February 1886.
29. Nova Scotia, *Debates,* 14 April 1886.
30. Fielding to Blake, 8 January 1886, Nos. 158-59, Fielding Papers.
31. Nova Scotia, *Debates,* 14 April 1886.
32. Fielding to Blake, 8 January 1886, Nos. 159-60, Fielding Papers.
33. Premier Fielding's Election Manifesto, 18 May 1886; reported in the *Morning Chronicle,* 26 May 1886.
34. Pictou *Colonial Standard,* 18 May 1886.
35. J.W. Carmichael to Blake, 17 May 1886, No. 405 Carmichael Papers, P.A.N.S.
36. Carmichael to Blake, 17 May 1886, No. 406, ibid.
37. *Morning Chronicle,* 18 May 1886.
38. New Glasgow *Eastern Chronicle,* 15 May 1886.
39. C.H. Tupper to Editor, London *Standard,* Charles Hibbert Tupper Correspondence (microfilm), 22 November 1886 (date of letter), P.A.N.S., P.A.C.
40. Carmichael to A.G. Jones, Carmichael Papers, 2 July 1886, No. 409, P.A.N.S.
41. Carmichael to Blake, 6 July 1886, No. 411, ibid.
42. "Nova Scotia's Case," Box 1, R.F. 2, Fielding Papers. This election handbill reveals the party's problems with repeal. Of thirty-eight items contained in the document, only four dealt with repeal.
43. Antigonish *Casket,* 10 February 1887.
44. Halifax *Morning Herald,* 12 February 1887.
45. D.G. Creighton, *John A. Macdonald: The Old Chieftain,* (Toronto, 1955), p. 469. The extent to which Nova Scotians looked upon the National Policy

with disfavour is open to question. As T.W. Acheson has demonstrated, the tariff—in its initial stages—encouraged industrial development in Nova Scotia. "Between 1881 and 1891," he writes, "the industrial growth of Nova Scotia outstripped all other provinces in eastern Canada." T.W. Acheson, "The National Policy and the Industrialization of the Maritimes, 1880-1910," *Acadiensis* (Spring 1972), p. 3.

46. *Morning Herald*, 15 January 1887.

47. In this regard, see Ernest Robert Forbes's excellent thesis, "The Rise and Fall of the Conservative Party in the Provincial Politics of Nova Scotia 1922-1933" (MA thesis, Dalhousie University, May 1967).

48. *Maritime Merchant*, 2 August 1923.

49. *Canadian Annual Review*, 1925-26, p. 396.

50. *Maritime Merchant*, 27 September 1923.

51. Province of Nova Scotia, *A Submission of its Claims with Respect to Maritime Disabilities within Confederation as Presented to the Royal Commission* (Halifax, 21 July 1926), pp. 117-139; and Norman McLeod Rogers, *A Submission on Dominion-Provincial Relations and the Fiscal Disabilities of Nova Scotia within the Canadian Federation* (Halifax, 1934), pp. 113-14.

52. Province of Nova Scotia, *A Submission With Respect to Maritime Disabilities*, p. 118.

53. *Canadian Annual Review*, 1924-25, p. 333. W.C. Milner wrote that "commercial and industrial life of 1924 proceeded along the same lines as in 1923. In most of the towns and villages lack of employment was severely felt, and, in consequence, in the early part of the year, there was a renewal of the exodus movement."

54. Kenneth McNaught, *A Prophet in Politics: A Biography of J.S. Woodsworth* (Toronto, 1959), pp. 173-79.

55. George E. Wilson to Hume Wrong, 26 March 1925, Nos. 138-40, Hume Wrong Papers, P.A.C.

56. W.H. Dennis to Arthur Meighen, 28 March 1925, Nos. 069424-6, Meighen Papers, P.A.C.

57. *Journals*, 1923, p. 262.

58. Forbes, "Rise and Fall of the Conservative Party," p. 206.

59. W.M. Robertson to W.S. Fielding, 2 February 1923, No. 58, G.F. Pearson Papers, P.A.N.S.

60. Rogers, *A Submission on Dominion-Provincial Relations*, pp. 32-33.

61. H. Blair Neatby, *William Lyon Mackenzie King, 1924-1932: The Lonely Heights* (Toronto, 1963), pp. 222-23.

62. Rogers, *A Submission on Dominion-Provincial Relations*, p. 110.

63. *The Jones Report on Nova Scotia's Economic Welfare within Confederation* (Halifax, 1934), p. 34.

64. *Submission by the Government of the Province of Nova Scotia to the Royal Commission on Dominion-Provincial Relations* (February 1938), p. 4.

65. Norman McLeod Rogers, "A Crisis of Federal Finance," *Canadian Forum*, (November 1934).

66. Norman McLeod Rogers, "The Progression of Loyalties," *Dalhousie Review*, (April 1931), p. 63.

List of Contributors

David Jay Bercuson,
Department of History, University of Calgary

Paul Phillips,
Department of Economics, University of Manitoba

Carman Miller,
Department of History, McGill University

Ernest R. Forbes,
Department of History, University of New Brunswick

T. W. Acheson,
Department of History, University of New Brunswick

T. D. Regehr,
Department of History, University of Saskatchewan

David E. Smith,
Department of Political Science, University of Saskatchewan

Colin D. Howell,
Department of History, St. Mary's University